ISLAND WALKS

The Western Isles, Skye and the Small Isles

ISLAND WALKS

The Western Isles, Skye and the Small Isles

STEPHEN WHITEHORNE

ILLUSTRATIONS BY HAMISH HASWELL-SMITH

Birlinn

First published in Great Britain in 2002 by
Birlinn Limited
West Newington House
10 Newington Road
Edinburgh EH9 1QS

www.birlinn.co.uk

ISBN 1 84158 213 1

British Library Cataloguing-in-Publication Data
A catalogue record for this book is available on request from the
British Library

Printed and bound in Spain by Book Print SL

Contents

Preface

Several years before I first visited the Hebrides I discovered images of them during my college years, in the early 1980s, in a book entitled *Tir a Mhurain* ('Land of the Bent Grass'). *Tir a Mhurain* is a poignant photographic study in black and white by the American photographer Paul Strand of the life, land and people of South Uist in 1954. Strand, credited with the distinction of being the first modernist photographer, was, undeniably, one of the grand masters of his craft. His three-month sojourn on South Uist, living with the people, sharing their hard work, poverty and happiness, was for him a kind of exile from the hostility and discomfort of McCarthyite America. The photographs he made are memorable for their honesty and humanity, and for their poetry: they speak more of a particular time and a place than any number of words could do. Published in 1962, the book is now very rare, having been out of print for several decades. So it was with great pleasure and some surprise that I chanced upon *Tir a Mhurain* again, in the township of Stoneybridge on my last visit to South Uist. Proudly dusting off her copy in the Post Office where she still worked, the 86-year-old postmistress, Mrs McRury, wedged the book open at the page showing a photograph of her late husband. She reminisced; we both chatted and drank endless cups of tea; roosters clucked through her kitchen and chased cats off the windowsills. Outside, machair flowers glittered and sparkled in the bright June sunshine. I had travelled thousands of island miles before reaching Stoneybridge, since art college. I had gone full circle it seemed and yet, maybe here, little had changed since Strand's time.

The Hebridean experience begins, if not from the bow of the Cal Mac ferry, then from that first step off the vessel on to the pier. For those of us returning to a familiar island, that first day is one of recognition – the feeling comes flooding back that, by having breached more than the obvious barrier of water, a different world has been re-entered, that in fact some other intangible and yet powerful frontier has been crossed. And the Hebrides are different worlds, each island individual, yet all sharing that same essential 'islandness'. Often some primeval craving is stirred by the inescapable proximity of the sea, by the surrounding seemingly endless ocean brimming with sights and sounds and responding to yet another configuration of wind and weather.

If forced to choose favourites, then there are three islands to which, more than any others, I am addicted. These islands are Mull, Colonsay and Barra. Your favourites may well be others because what you find depends on who you are and when you are there, on manner, attitude and perception. For 'islophiles', island-hopping can be every bit as obsessive as Munro collecting is among summit-bagging hill-walkers. But rather than name-ticking away as many islands as you can in a week or two's holiday, you will find that exploring just one or two islands in the same period is usually time better spent.

When we go out into the countryside for recreation, some of us go as soldiers, others as poets. Some may climb a hill as a gazelle might, while others do so with the grace of a yeti. Whatever our varied reasons and our eccentric ways, we invariably return changed in some way, usually for the better. In the islands, that transformation is, as it was for Paul Strand, likely to be profound. Do not be tempted to rush through the Hebrides.

Stephen Whitehorne

Acknowledgments

The people who have been generous in their help in putting this guide together are probably greater in number than the totality of the Hebridean islands. For their invaluable assistance in devising walks and for making my island experiences so memorable, a few names need special mention. But the list is all too brief, which is more a reflection on my inexcusable inability to remember names than for my lack of gratitude to those not mentioned.

For her patience during my countless wanderings beyond the mainland, and for her continued love and support throughout, I am indebted to Virginie. Long after a return from the last island, as the manuscript deadline loomed, she yet again spared me the torture of two-finger typing. I take for granted neither her exceptional keyboard skills nor her success in preventing my slide into domestic chaos. Thank you for always being there.

I hope that one day I am able to repay the generosity of Anne and Roy Robinson at Portnalong on Skye, in welcoming me into their home. Also on Skye, thanks to Ian at the Bay View Guest House, Talisker, a mine of information on the area and brewer of the best nettle beer in the British Isles. And to the Broadford-to-Elgol postbus driver, whose name eludes me, but for his tales of Bonnie Prince Charlie and his own TV fame with a BBC camera crew, I shall not forget, and, for guiding me to the right people on Rum, Lorne Gill of Scottish Natural Heritage.

Conversing with so many people, each with a unique knowledge of a local place and its history has profoundly enhanced my experience of the Hebrides. Margaret Moodie at the Raasay Heritage Museum, Robert MacGillivray on Benbecula, the lobster fisherman of Baleshare, Ian Maciomhair of Loch Erisart Ltd, Stornoway, and the archaeology students from Cardiff University on South Uist, have all been most forthcoming in this respect. My close friend Simon Mootz, ex-Scottish Wildlife Trust Warden on Handa, was also a great help in offering information on that island.

As alluded to in my Preface, one of my fondest memories whilst travelling in the islands was the company of Mary McRury on South Uist. She still runs the tiny Post Office at Stoneybridge. After six cups of tea and hours of chat, I left, having been relieved of a £5 note for a pair of hand-knitted socks, which probably makes it the longest yet most enjoyable sales pitch ever.

Finally, I thank Hugh Andrew, my publisher, for his guidance, and numerous contacts, but most importantly for his enthusiasm for everything Hebridean.

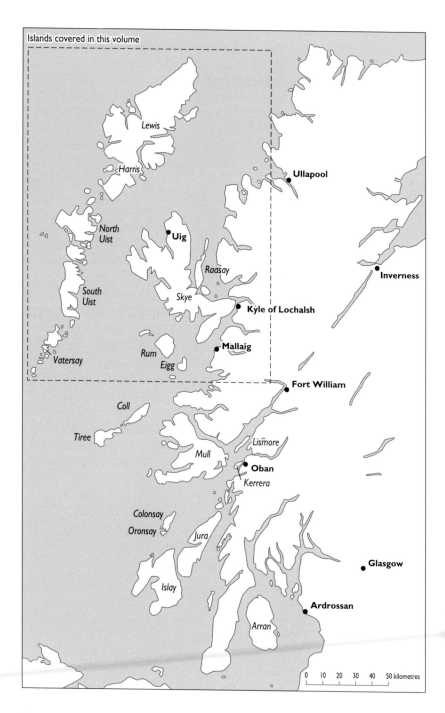

Islands covered in this volume

Lewis

Harris

Ullapool

North Uist

Uig

Raasay

Inverness

South Uist

Skye

Kyle of Lochalsh

Vatersay

Rum

Eigg

Mallaig

Fort William

Coll

Tiree

Lismore

Mull

Oban

Kerrera

Colonsay

Oronsay

Jura

Glasgow

Islay

Ardrossan

Arran

0 10 20 30 40 50 kilometres

The Northern Hebrides

There are well over 100 inhabited and uninhabited islands off the west coast of Scotland, that is, detached landmasses surrounded by sea water. Although this guide covers in detail just ten of them, they collectively represent much of the total land area of the Northern Hebrides. Those chosen have been selected on the basis of ease of access and the potential for exploring on foot the best of the islands' scenery and wildlife. Consequently, the larger, more populated islands are included, which also tend to be the more frequently visited. Other smaller islands of interest, but for which no walks are suggested, are briefly described in Other Islands to Visit (Chapter 8). Those not mentioned at all are those that are so difficult of access as to be rarely visited except perhaps by people lucky enough to have their own boats.

The word 'Hebrides' derives from the Norse word *Havbredey*, meaning 'islands on the edge of the sea', for this was the perception of Scotland's detached west-coast landmasses to the seafaring Viking invaders of the first millennium AD. The mental maps of their domain, a world seen through the eyes of a race of colonising mariners, would invariably have seen land in the context of the ocean rather than in any way like our modern land-centred view of the world. The Hebrides, for most of us these days, are islands located on the northwest edge of Europe rather than a group of viable landmasses easily accessible by galley.

Hopping from island to island in your own vessel, and at your own pace, is an option for sailors and undoubtedly adds to the pleasure of discovery. Most visitors, however, have to rely on the Caledonian MacBrayne vehicle and passenger ferry services to reach their chosen island destinations. Once there, visitors discover that the Scottish Islands are ideal for outdoor pursuits of all kinds, from sailing, climbing and windsurfing to fishing, bird-watching and painting.

People visit the Hebrides for many reasons, although walking is now recognised as the most popular leisure-time activity in Scotland. Without doubt, the best way to see most of what the islands have to offer is on foot. For this reason, this guidebook outlines the Hebridean experience from the point of view of the walker, with the assumption that, on the bigger islands at least, access to private transport is possible. However, public transport options are also indicated.

In choosing the walks described, my aim was to cover those with the finest scenery and the most interesting historical sites and monuments as well as some of the best opportunities for observing wildlife possible in Britain. This is not a guide for the 'Scoutmaster' school of exploring (although a few quite strenuous mountain expeditions have been included), nor is it for 'collectors' or 'name-tickers'. Instead, the walks are for those who wish to explore at a pace appropriate to Hebridean tranquillity and rhythms: ramblers who wish to visit specific places of interest, lingerers seeking to absorb and reflect upon their surroundings, and curious hedge-pokers who perhaps want to discover something new and fascinating about an island.

This book is one of two volumes and covers the northern half of the Hebrides, the islands north of, and including, Eigg. My hope is that with these 25 walks and 26 short walks I have achieved as full and as complete a representation of the northern Hebrides as is possible within this limited number of pages.

CHAPTER 2

Practical Information

The first port of call prior to any trip to the islands (after this book) should be the Scottish Tourist Board in Edinburgh or the relevant regional tourist board. They can supply the appropriate brochures listing accommodation, essential services, tours, etc. The islands included in this guide are covered by two regional tourist boards: for the Small Isles and Skye, but not including the Outer Hebrides, contact the Highland and Islands Tourist Board. For destinations in the Outer Hebrides, contact the Western Isles Tourist Board. All the bigger, more popular islands have tourist information offices, usually located in the main town, although opening times may be seasonal.

For information on ferry travel between the islands and to and from the mainland, contact Caledonian MacBrayne for timetables and fares. Flights to the Western Isles from Glasgow and Inverness can be booked through British Airways.

For the addresses and telephone numbers of the above and other relevant organisations, see Appendix 2.

HEBRIDEAN WEATHER AND WHEN TO GO

One word best describes the weather on the west side of Scotland: unpredictable. The region is influenced by fronts constantly rolling in off the Atlantic, which, despite what you may have seen in the Mediterranean-style photographs used in tourist brochures, keep the climate predominantly cool and moist. Were it not so, the Hebrides would undoubtedly be a more popular destination. Very cold temperatures, however, are rare, because of the moderating effect of the Gulf Stream, the warm ocean current that flows across the Atlantic from the Gulf of Mexico, which means that on islands such as Eigg palm trees can be seen growing in luxuriant gardens. Frosts and prolonged falls of snow are unusual but then so too are hot summer days.

The weather can vary greatly across the Hebrides. Mountainous islands such as Skye and Rum attract clouds like magnets and receive considerably more rainfall than low-lying islands just a few miles away. Wind is more or less a constant feature of the weather on the islands, continually blasting and reshaping coastal sand dunes, often stirring up turbulent seas and typically buffeting hilltops with unrelenting vigour.

Big dramatic skies and changing cloudscapes can add to the excitement of walking in the Hebrides, and the clarity of the air can give spells of exceptional visibility. When the wind drops and the sky turns blue over a sheltered shell-sand beach, when the sea turns turquoise on one side of the pale dunes and the machair sparkles in the sunlight with floral colour on the other, it will seem there are few places in the world more perfect.

Weather patterns of recent years suggest that May to mid-June and September are when the longest and driest spells of settled weather occur. Avoiding the islands during the summer has the added benefit of escaping the peak tourist season, the highest prices and the worst of the midges. For the landscapes of islands with plenty of trees, autumn heralds a palette of delightful colour while winter snow can transform the Skye Cuillin into a sparkling jewel. The choice is yours.

TRAVELLING TO THE ISLANDS AND PUBLIC TRANSPORT

All the islands that have been included in this guidebook can be reached by scheduled ferry services. The majority of these services, to the larger islands at least, are operated by Caledonian MacBrayne (Cal Mac) whose vehicle and passenger ferries operate from the mainland ports of Oban, Mallaig and Ullapool. For the Western Isles there is also a service from Uig (Skye), and other smaller operators serve on routes to the less visited islands. Private charter is also sometimes an option. Frequency of ferry services to the islands varies with their remoteness, size and population, and on most routes is significantly reduced out of season, between October and April. Disruption to services is possible during spells of bad weather.

Barra, Benbecula and Lewis are among the Hebridean destinations that have airports. These islands are served by daily British Airways Express flights from Glasgow and/or Inverness.

Having reached your destination, travelling around is made a good deal less problematic by the use of your own vehicle, especially on the larger islands. If you are using the Cal Mac services, ferrying a car between the islands can become a costly exercise, but without wheels, your flexibility is invariably compromised. On the smaller islands, however, where distances are not great and there are not many roads, a private vehicle is not so essential.

Bus services vary greatly from island to island, from reliable and regular services to none at all. Private minibuses, taxis and Royal Mail postbuses can, in some places, fill in where other services are lacking, although these operators normally coincide with ferry times only. It is also important to note that throughout the islands most public transport is non-existent on a Sunday, whether ferry, bus or aeroplane. There are no main-line rail services on any Scottish island.

More detailed information pertaining to specific **ACCESS** and **PUBLIC TRANSPORT** services for a particular island are given at the beginning of each island section.

ACCOMMODATION

Like public transport, accommodation on the islands varies with remoteness, size and population. Popular islands such as Skye have an infinite number of possibilities, from luxury hotels to bothies, while on largely uninhabited and little-visited islands the choice may be limited to one hotel or a couple of bed and breakfasts.

Only a sparse scattering of Scottish Youth Hostel Association hostels are to be found in the Hebrides, often in surprisingly inconvenient locations. In the Outer Hebrides these are run by the Gatliff Hebridean Hostels Trust. Independent bunkhouses are increasingly supplementing the budget accommodation market. Like hostels, bunkhouses are well suited to walkers, are normally run by people with a good knowledge of the local environment, and most have drying areas. They are good places for meeting people but a bad choice when you are deprived of sleep by the sound of others snoring.

Camping is obviously the cheapest option of all, although only a few official campsites are to be found on the islands. Wild camping on the coast or in the hills is another possibility, although permission should be sought from the local farmer or landowner.

Most of the islands in this book have at least one hotel. Bed and breakfast (B&B) accommodation, however, in private homes and guesthouses is undoubtedly the most widespread option. They vary in quality, beds are not always comfortable but breakfasts are invariably substantial. For an average B&B, expect to pay £18-£28 per person per night.

Self-catering cottage and caravan accommodation is an appropriate choice for a group of people staying on one island for a week or more. They can also be a very economical option, with a security and privacy advantage over hostels and more flexibility regarding meal times than either B&Bs or hotels.

Specific details regarding the available **ACCOMMODATION** on each island is given at the beginning of each island section.

FINDING FOOD, DRINK AND FUEL

On some islands, finding food is not always easy, whether this be bar or restaurant food or shop food for preparing your own meals. In the more remote places there may be just one hotel for bar meals (probably also the only place to drink alcohol on the island) and possibly one island grocery store that often doubles as the post office. One of the first things to establish on arriving is the opening times of such places; they are often very restricted.

A particular annoyance for hill-walkers after a long tiring tramp is the impossibility of a bar or restaurant meal after 8.30 p.m. or 9 p.m. Foreign visitors, in particular, find this frustrating. Certainly, it has to be said that no other nation in Europe would tolerate such restrictive eating times. Few, if any, grocery stores are open on a Sunday, and the same goes for petrol stations, so keep an eye on that fuel gauge. Respect for the Sabbath is part of the Hebridean experience.

Although in a few places things have improved significantly in the past ten years or so, the Hebrides are not generally known for their cuisine. It seems a kind of irony of commerce that the seas around the islands still produce some of the finest seafood in the world, and yet, with the exception of farmed salmon, most of this is now exported to France, Spain and Portugal. Take advantage of fresh fish, fruit and vegetables where you find them. Vegetarians in particular may have a difficult time.

Be prepared to pay much higher prices for both food and fuel than on the mainland as almost everything has to be imported.

APPROPRIATE CLOTHING AND EQUIPMENT

Whatever time of year you choose to visit the Hebrides, be prepared to encounter all four seasons, sometimes in a single day. Do not waste valuable luggage space on smart town clothes: occasions for dressing up will be few and far between. Apart from normal casual wear, pack with practical considerations in mind: waterproofs, walking boots, warm hat, thick socks, fleece or jumper, thermals, gloves and warm trousers. Jeans are not a good idea because when they get wet, they get heavy, lose their thermal capacity and take ages to dry out. In summer add shorts, sun hat, sunglasses and sun cream to the list. Moisturiser and lip balm are also useful as a good day out on the islands typically means a wind-chapped sunburnt face. Even late autumn sunlight, when reflected off the sea, can be deceptively powerful.

Walking boots, or Wellington boots, are the normal footwear just about wherever you go: just take a look at the locals. Walking boots are certainly essential if you intend to do any serious walking, as are all the above-mentioned items of clothing. For walks of more than three or four hours' duration, a small rucksack containing additional items including the relevant Ordnance Survey map and food and water should be carried. A basic first-aid kit is a wise precaution too.

If you are heading up on to the mountains, you should also carry a compass, whistle, watch, torch, bivvy (survival) bag and emergency food rations (see also SAFETY CONSIDERATIONS AND MOUNTAIN RESCUE below).

ACCESS FOR WALKERS

When walking in the Hebrides, using waymarked, established or well-maintained footpaths is the exception rather than the rule. As in the Highlands, traversing wet, rough and unpathed terrain is often the norm. In general, this does not cause a problem for landowners although it is important for walkers to respect estate needs.

Forestry, deerstalking, grouse shooting, lambing and other farming and crofting practices are the principal activities that might restrict the movements of walkers in the islands, particularly in the mountain areas. Land in the ownership of the Forestry Commission, the National Trust for Scotland and National Nature Reserves under the auspices of Scottish Natural Heritage are, with the exception of deer study areas on Rum, normally unaffected.

The deerstalking season begins in mid-August and, with the culling of hinds, can last until early February. However, precise times may vary from estate to estate, so always consult locally. With specific regard to the areas and walks outlined in the book, those where temporary restricted access may be imposed for stalking are in the Forest of Harris on North Harris (Walk 23 and Short Walk 22).

The grouse-shooting season is from 12 August, 'the glorious 12th', until 10 December, and similar restrictions on access to land may apply then, although few islands have managed grouse moors. Between March and May, it is important to avoid disturbing sheep during lambing. Sheep fencing on farm and coastal croft land may prove an annoyance for walkers but rarely presents a serious obstruction. In describing the walks, I have done my best to avoid routes that cross fencing although, of course, the boundaries of fields and enclosures are forever shifting.

SAFETY CONSIDERATIONS AND MOUNTAIN RESCUE

When out on long walks in remote areas, and certainly when heading into the mountains, if possible avoid going alone and always leave written word of your route and report your return. Always carry a map and compass and be certain you know how to use them. Take a torch or whistle as, if you get into trouble, the mountain distress signals are six long whistle blasts or torch flashes, repeated at one-minute intervals. Continue to repeat the distress signals until your rescuers are with you. The recognised answer is three whistle blasts or torch flashes.

A mobile phone can be useful in the event of an emergency, or otherwise it is vital that one of the party gets down to a phone immediately. If you need the rescue services, dial 999 and ask for the police. Follow the instructions you receive. Only on Skye do Mountain Rescue posts and facilities exist, so elsewhere the rescue services may take longer to arrive. On the other islands, therefore, the preventive measures outlined above are even more vital.

MIDGES

Culicoides impunctatus (the Highland midge) is barely two millimetres long but is often present in ferocious swarms, nowhere more so than on the islands of Rum and Skye. Some people come up in huge red itchy blotches when bitten by these tiny insects; they are quite capable of evicting susceptible humans from the Hebridean islands altogether. They breed in soggy sphagnum moss and peaty acid soils, so mountain regions tend to be the worst affected. Overcast days and nights between June and September are when they are most active. They are blown away by the wind, which is probably why west-facing coasts seem relatively free of them and perhaps why red deer head towards hilltops in the summer time. Effective defence comes in the form of citronella (natural) or Jungle Formula (chemical) repellents. When camping out in the summer, a midge net may be essential.

CHAPTER 3

How to Use this Guide

In this guide I have set out to achieve as straightforward and reader-friendly a layout as possible. This book is divided into eight chapters. The chapters preceding this one deal with factual and practical information especially useful to those unfamiliar with the islands. Chapters 4 to 6 are intended to give an overall context to the Hebrides, information that I hope will provide a useful, if basic, background knowledge. It might of course also be referred to while actually out on the ground pursuing the walks.

The main 'meat' of the guide is in Chapter 7, which gives detailed route information on a total of 25 walks and 26 short walks on nine separate islands. Each island section includes a description of at least one or more main walks as well as, in most cases, a few shorter walks. I have carefully researched, tried and tested all the walks.

Chapter 8 briefly outlines a few other islands in the northern islands for which no walks have been suggested but which are nonetheless well worth visiting, especially for those with specialised interests such as bird-watching or geology.

A glossary of frequently occurring Gaelic terms, as well as the names and addresses of relevant travel companies and organisations are listed in the appendices.

INTRODUCTIONS TO EACH ISLAND

Even before first picking up this book, you might well already have decided on your island destinations. If not, then study the introductions to each of the islands in Chapter 7. The first part of the text for each island gives a brief overview, general information in respect of topography, history, natural history and main points of interest. Following that, more specific information pertaining to the **MAIN SETTLEMENTS**, means of **ACCESS**, **ACCOMMODATION** options (with some contact telephone numbers), **PUBLIC TRANSPORT** services and the relevant **ORDNANCE SURVEY LANDRANGER MAPS** for a particular island is given under separate subheadings.

All the main tourist attractions, notably landscape features and archaeological sites to be found on an island, are listed at the end of each island introduction under the sub-heading **MAIN PLACES OF INTEREST**. Each place of interest has been allocated a number that corresponds to a location on the relevant island map. This location (and its number) also appears in **bold**, when mentioned and/or visited within the walk descriptions. Those places of interest that are not on the route of any of the walks are instead described briefly within the listing and can normally be visited without wandering too far from a car.

CHOOSING A WALK

Your choice of walk will, to a large extent, depend on your personal interests. But given the wild and remote nature of many of the islands, there are of course other factors to consider. Logistics, such as the convenience of reaching a starting point, the time that is available and, as always in Scotland, the prevailing weather conditions, will all influence your decision. It would obviously be unwise, as well as unrewarding, to consider a mountain walk if the summits are obscured by cloud, for instance (see **SAFETY CONSIDERATIONS** in Chapter 2).

The map for each island clearly identifies the location of the main walks on that particular island. Grid references are given, where necessary, in the walk descriptions. Short Walks are not shown, but all short walks are less than $2^1/_2$ hours' duration. In devising the main walks, I applied just a few constraints with convenience and safety in mind, which are that a walk must:

- start and finish from the same parking place.
- be able to be completed by walkers of reasonable fitness within $6^1/_2$ hours (yet be of greater duration than $2^1/_2$ hours). None is intended to be a marathon and even the shortest winter day should be long enough to complete the longest walk.
- require no rock-climbing abilities or the use of a rope, even on mountains.
- offer alternative 'easy' options on all walks that may involve some scrambling.

INTRODUCTION TO EACH WALK

The text for the description of each walk is preceded by a brief summary of useful information relating to that walk. The following table indicates what kind of information is given under each heading:

Main interest and sights	A single sentence briefly outlining the interest, followed by a list of the highlights of the walk in the order that they are encountered; their numbers relate to a location on the general island map and also correspond to an alphabetical listing under the subheading MAIN PLACES OF INTEREST. They appear in bold in the walk descriptions.
Route	The walks fall into one of two categories: **circular** - starting and finishing at the same location and roughly circular in design. **linear** - a there-and-back walk, returning by the outward route.
Grade	All the walks have been allocated a grade on the following basis: **easy** - mostly following well-defined, level and dry footpaths and tracks and less than $3^1/_2$ hours' duration. **easy/moderate** - mostly following well-defined footpaths and tracks but with possibly some easy gradients and less than $4^1/_2$ hours' duration. **moderate** - possibly involving some easy hillwalking on low hills or perhaps the traverse of unpathed terrain or perhaps an easily traversed but long walk. **moderate/strenuous** - normally involving significant gradient or some hillwalking and often on rough terrain but of no real difficulty other than physical exertion. **strenuous** - suitable only for experienced hillwalkers or fit individuals with capable companions.

Normally long walks, involving steep climbs, most often traversing unpathed terrain; attaining heights and situations where navigational skills would be essential in adverse weather.

Map The relevant Ordnance Survey Landranger sheet, with map number or numbers given. It is always a good idea to carry the right map.

Starting point This is usually a convenient parking place; a six-figure map reference is also given.

Finishing point This will be the same location as the starting point.

Distance Distances given are to the nearest 0.1 km/$^1/_4$ mi (duration of the walk to nearest $^1/_4$ hour - includes short rest stops).

Paths and terrain This gives an indication of whether or not defined paths exist, the condition of path and tracks, whether any tarmac is traversed, the nature of the terrain, an assessment of the gradients to be encountered and any likely obstacles or difficulties.

Options Curtailments and escape routes as well as possible extensions to the main walk are suggested as options. Necessary adjustments to grade and duration of the walk appear between brackets.

Nearby walks All nearby main walks and short walks are given, that is, other walks within about 6 km/$3^3/_4$ mi of the starting point.

Refreshments This gives the location of possible 'pit-stops' for food and drink, such as hotel bars, cafés and shops, although few walks pass such places en route. Where none exists, the nearest to the starting point is given.

USING THE MAPS
• The individual walk maps are intended to show the general route of the walk only. They are rough and not suitable for navigation; always carry the relevant OS maps.

- All landmarks, archaeological sites and attractions for each island appear on the walk maps by name and on the island maps by number and corresponding to that feature listed under **MAIN PLACES OF INTEREST**. Many of these highlights also appear in the text of the walks, as they are encountered.
- The route of a walk is shown in red on the relevant walk map.
- Arrows on the walk map show the direction of the walk.
- All essential features are marked on the walk maps, including the starting point, appropriate lochs, rivers and burns, and prominent hills, roads and buildings.
- Munros and other mountain summits are shown in the following way
  ▲ Munro
- △ Other mountain summit

ABBREVIATIONS

To avoid constant repetitions, a limited number of abbreviations have been used in the route descriptions:

Cal Mac Caledonian MacBrayne

FC	Forestry Commission
ft	feet
GR	grid reference (six figure)
km	kilometres
m	metre(s)
mi	mile(s)
NSA	National Scenic Area
OS	Ordnance Survey
OSLR	Ordnance Survey Landranger (map)
NNR	National Nature Reserve
NTS	National Trust for Scotland
RSPB	Royal Society for the Protection of Birds
SNH	Scottish Natural Heritage
SSSI	Special Site of Scientific Interest
SWT	Scottish Wildlife Trust
SYHA	Scottish Youth Hostels Association
trig	trigonometrical

CHAPTER 4

Natural History and Geology

The geology of the islands is very complex, and throughout the Hebrides a remarkable variety of rocks, both in terms of type and age, can be seen. Episodes of rock-forming and archipelago-building span hundreds of millions of years and the result is some of the most spectacular landscapes in Europe.

Movements of ice up to about 10,000 years ago have further sculpted the rocks and given rise to features shared by many of the islands. Sharply cut mountain arêtes and corries, U-shaped valleys, glacial erratics and raised beaches have all helped form the many and varied landscapes of the Hebrides. Raised beaches, caused by a rebounding of the land after the weight of ice had disappeared, are a recurring feature of many coastal walks.

The Hebrides have a very long history of geological activity, an unimaginable time scale in which the landmasses that constitute present-day Scotland and her islands have spent much of their time south of the equator. In the Outer Hebrides, a grey, sparkling metamorphic rock of igneous origin, known as gneiss, constitutes many of the landscape features. Lewisian gneiss is one of the oldest rocks on the planet, having been formed under intense heat and pressure nearly three billion years ago, long before any kind of life appeared on the earth. Unfortunately, precisely because it is such an impermeable rock, a number of the Hebridean islands are now back on the agenda as potential sites for a permanent underground dump for Britain's growing stockpile of radioactive waste.

Islands such as Skye and Rum are quite distinctly mountainous in character. Among the very highest ranges are those made up of igneous rocks. On Skye the hills are formed from magma that cooled slowly under the surface whereas those on Rum resulted from volcanic activity. An exception are the mountains of Harris, which are almost entirely of Lewisian gneiss (metamorphosed granite). The sharp and shapely Black Cuillin of Skye is formed of hard black gabbro and constitutes the finest range of mountains in the British Isles. Undoubtedly, one of the most impressive of all volcanic outcrops occurs on Eigg, with the towering wedge of pitchstone that has formed An Sgurr (Walk 1). The extinct volcano on Rum exhibits unusual igneous layering, but perhaps the weirdest formations of basalt are to be seen at Trotternish on Skye, below The Storr (Walk 9) and at the Quiraing (Walk 10).

Sedimentary rocks feature much less visibly in the Hebrides than either igneous or metamorphic types, having not survived so well the long succession of geological upheavals. Handa, which is of Torridonian sandstone, is a notable exception.

Geology plays an essential part in affecting the interest and diversity of an island's natural history. Geographical position, climate and the activities of human beings are other factors. Soon after the last Ice Age, many of the Hebrides would have supported extensive forests: in some islands predominantly Scots pine and oak and in other, windier, more exposed places, such as St Kilda, birch and hazel scrub.

Widespread destruction of Hebridean forests began when the first Neolithic farmers began clearing areas for settlement, for the growing of crops and for grazing. In this way, biodiversity would, up to a point, have actually increased and the tapestry of forest and open areas that developed would have been good for wildlife. But populations grew rapidly and the demand for timber became insatiable, resulting in accelerated forest destruction when, at the same time, around the second millennium BC, the climate also turned cooler and wetter. Eventually, the fertile top soil was lost, peat was dug for fuel and sheep were introduced, thus further devastating the landscape and creating an environment essentially hostile to forest regeneration.

The Hebridean landscape today is characterised by a stark and desolate kind of beauty, although some islands are noticeably more wooded than others. Among the trees to be observed in the northern Hebrides are a few unexpected species, such as the large woodlands of ash on the Sleat peninsula of Skye and palm trees in the sheltered corners of Eigg. Subtropical species find a foothold, not because of high temperatures but because of the lack of winter frosts as a result of the moderating effect of the Gulf Stream. The Outer Hebrides however, are almost entirely devoid of trees.

In some instances, human intervention has been positive for plants and wildlife. The machair that fringes the Atlantic beaches of the Western Isles is unique in terms of the rich plant and birdlife it sustains. *Machair* is a Gaelic word that describes the flat, grassy coastal plain formed by the drifting of fine shell sand from the beaches on to the peaty ground just behind the dunes. This intermixing has a liming effect on the peat, creating a fertile natural grassland that in summer is host to a stunning display of colourful wild flowers. Generations of crofters have worked the machair for agriculture, ploughing in seaweed to bind and fertilise the sand, adding manure through grazing and traditionally cropping small patches on a rotational basis. These practices have further enhanced the wildlife interest. According to the crofters of South Uist, the most attractive flower displays are to be seen two years after the machair has been worked for potatoes. It is then that daisies, buttercups, bird's-foot trefoil, wild pansies, poppies, clovers, purple-tufted vetch and other wild flowers in their thousands produce a spectacularly beautiful carpet of colour. Of orchids alone, a total of twenty-seven different species are known to grow on the machair. In the meadows set farther back from the dunes (on the Uists, the marshy ground fringing a coastal string of freshwater lochs) flourishes a wetland type of machair, where conditions give rise to a rich mix of damp-loving wild flowers, including bogbeam, northern marsh orchids, ragged-robin, kingcups and cow parsley. This is ideal habitat for one of Britain's rarest birds, the corncrake. Encouraging traditional crofting techniques, such as the late mowing of hay, has helped corncrakes to nest successfully and to make something of a comeback in recent years.

The vibrant colours of summer behind the dunes is in striking contrast to the grey, rock-intruded landscapes of the rather drab ochres and browns of the moorlands and blanket bogs. A rugged, mountainous spine extends right along the east side of the Long Isle – spectacular scenery but where little more than rough grasses, heathers and mosses survive in sparse acid soils. The lowland peatlands of Lewis, however, are an internationally rare habitat supporting a unique range of flora and fauna. Insect-eating plants such as sundews and butterwort thrive here, and divers, dunlin and greenshank are among the breeding birds.

In places where the movements of red deer have been restricted, a greater number of plants are able to survive. On the island of Rum, for example, vast mountain areas are now being managed with the aim of extending the diversity of the upland flora. Whilst on islands with a bedrock primarily of the sedimentary type, its associated plant life is likely to be different again. But if there is one flowering plant to be seen in reasonable abundance throughout the Hebrides, it is the yellow iris (yellow flag). Tall, attractive and proliferating on damp ground, June is the best time to see it in flower.

Although the Hebrides have much to occupy the botanist, it is perhaps for the bird life that the islands are most frequently visited by naturalists. The Hebrides are renowned for their colonies of sea birds, the most spectacular in Europe. Among the gull species present are the herring gull, kittiwake, fulmar and black-backed gull while the auks are well represented by guillemots, razorbills and puffins. Shags, cormorants and skuas are also fairly numerous. The remote St Kilda group has more seabirds than any other island group in Britain, notably on Stac Lee, the largest gannetry in the northern hemisphere, while the mountains of Rum prove ideal territory for the nest burrows of thousands of Manx shearwaters. Not surprisingly, many nesting birds favour sea-cliff sanctuaries on remote, sparsely inhabited or uninhabited archipelagos such as the Treshnish Isles, Handa and North Rona.

A number of islands are of national and international importance for their birds. North Uist supports large numbers of ground-nesting birds such as dunlin, redshank, lapwing and ringed plover while Loch Driudibeg on South Uist is important for its numbers of native greylag geese. And not forgetting of course, the ubiquitous and unmissable oystercatcher, bombarding you repeatedly on every beach and shore and screaming 'cleach, cleach': the only bird, it seems, that speaks Gaelic. Two very notable wildlife success stories in recent years have been the increase in numbers of corncrake in its stronghold on the Western Isles and the reintroduction of the white-tailed sea eagle. Since the first releases of eaglets on Rum on 1975, these huge and magnificent birds of prey have bred successfully and extended their range to other islands. Among the eagles, however, golden eagles are a more frequent sight, with a good concentration of territories in the Harris mountains. Peregrine falcon, hen harrier and kestrel are among the other birds of prey to be seen on the islands.

In the seas around the islands, marine mammals are also plentiful. Grey seals bobbing on the waves or basking on the rocks are a common sight, with ten per cent of the world population gathering every autumn in the Monach Isles, just off North Uist. Otters also seem to favour the west coast of Scotland and her island shores as a habitat. Telltale dorsal fins breaking water one after the other betray the presence of porpoises or dolphins on a feeding frenzy among a shoal of mullet or mackerel. Whales also frequent Hebridean seas: from the bigger islands in summer you can join a whale-watching tour to look for minke whales or even killer whales.

Land mammals are generally less easy to spot, except perhaps in mountain areas such as on Rum and Harris. Here, the red deer, Britain's largest land mammal, is relatively common thanks to the extermination of the wolf, its natural predator, as well as through the active encouragement of their numbers on sporting estates. Raasay is the only place in the Hebrides where pine martens are to be found, while ecological isolation on many islands has produced a number of unique subspecies of rodent, including the St Kilda mouse, the Rum mouse and the Raasay bank vole.

CHAPTER 5

Settlement and Archaeological Sites

When Scotland's seas and landmasses were finally released from the grip of ice about 10,000 years ago, a warmer climate allowed extensive forests to become established. The earliest evidence of a human presence yet discovered in the Hebrides stretches back to the forest dwellers of some 8,000 years ago, with the discovery of Mesolithic shell and bone refuse tips and antler fish spears on Rum and Oronsay. Surviving by a nomadic existence, these people from the south pushed north in the search for ever richer hunting grounds in the post-glacial forests, rivers and seas. It is possible that they were preceded by Palaeolithic peoples of an earlier age, although no such evidence has been found in Scotland.

Neolithic tribes continued to push northwards, with the first farmers arriving on the islands about 6,000 years ago. These later Stone Age people came with new ideas and began to clear the trees and establish settlements. Replacing the hunter-gatherers and their ceaseless search for food, the incomers began farming crops and breeding cattle. Forest clearance was necessary to release land suitable for such practices, the first steps in creating the characteristic moorland landscape of much of the Highlands and islands we see today. By applying agricultural resourcefulness in respect of acquiring food, time was made available for other concerns.

The earliest of the prehistoric structures to be found in the islands are the **chambered cairns** of about 3000 BC, North Uist having the greatest concentration with the best-preserved example in the islands at Barpa Langass (Short Walk 18). Five thousand years after their construction, these sometimes huge stone tombs remain a distinctive feature of the Hebridean landscape. They form two main types: passage graves and gallery graves, predating even the Egyptian pyramids. These communal burial places suggest a religious preoccupation and a belief in the afterlife long before the arrival of Christianity.

Perhaps the most awe-inspiring structures of prehistory with spiritual significance, however, are the mysterious **standing stones** and **stone circles** that began appearing in the Hebrides about 4,000 years ago. Their exact purpose remains uncertain, but in the arrangements of their stones, evidence of certain astronomical alignments is a typical feature. In one way or another, stone circles must have played an important part in rituals, as their construction would have been a massive commitment of time and energy. Callanish on Lewis (Short Walk 24) has the finest examples of stone circles in Scotland. Their builders were of the early Bronze Age, the first in Britain to utilise metal in replacing stone tools and weapons. Late Bronze Age people fashioned distinctive beaker pottery and were thus known as the 'Beaker people'.

From about 600 BC there followed successive waves of Celtic settlers from Central Europe, steadily increasing the population along the coastal fringes of northern Britain. Warfare was endemic among villages then, to secure control of essential resources and thus further driving the new technologies in metalworking for more effective tools and weapons. The men of iron succeeded 'the men of bronze', bringing with them ever more complex and elaborate skills in working metal. The stone work seen in their distinctive circular structures in the form of **brochs** and **duns**, built between 300 BC and AD 200, shows them to be equally adept stone masons. These defensive units were built possibly to guard against the Roman threat. Unique to Britain, numerous Iron Age brochs and duns are scattered throughout the islands, and many were reoccupied in later centuries, testimony, perhaps, to the quality of their original construction and also to the superb vantage points that they occupied, normally to the sea. Dun an Sticer in North Uist, for instance, was only finally abandoned in the early seventeenth century. Dun Carloway Broch on Lewis is the best-preserved example in the Hebrides, showing well the galleried walls over three metres thick at the base, with staircases and storage areas in between. Duns were somewhat smaller dry-stone defensive structures.

Although the Romans never reached the Hebrides, they encountered unruly Iron Age tribes on their frequent incursions in mainland Scotland and named them the Picti, or Picts, meaning 'painted people', whom they despised as well as feared. Scotland derived its name from the 'Scotti', Celtic people who arrived from Ireland in the fifth century and who occupied the Hebrides and the West of Scotland. Christianity came to the islands in AD 563, when St Columba landed on Iona.

Within 200 years of St Columba another round of bloodletting had begun, this time initiated from the north, with the Viking invasions. The Norsemen have a well-recorded reputation as a brutal race of pillaging raiders, but they were also exceptionally skilled mariners and great innovators. Inventors of the keel and the rudder, they were able to make much of northern Scotland and the Hebrides their own. Early raids proved them to be ruthless pirates and rampant territorial expansionists. By the end of the eighth century, however, they had begun to settle and assimilate with the natives, creating a

Celtic-Norse ethnic mix, especially in the Northern Isles and the Western Isles. Even today many place names retain their Norse origins.

The Vikings brought with them a village lifestyle and have left some evidence of longhouses (similar to traditional blackhouses), but overall they left little in the way of archaeological relics. The most famous Norse find of all is the Lewis Chessmen (Walk 24). The Norse kings had their grip on the Hebrides for over 300 years until, in the twelfth century, a Scots chief, Somerled, rose against them. At Finlaggan on Islay, Somerled had established a dynasty that became known as the 'Lordship of the Isles', and his grandson, Donald of Islay, gave his name to the clan Donald. The MacDonalds went on to become the most powerful of clans. With the Treaty of Perth, Norse control was finally severed in 1266.

The archaeological legacy of the medieval period in the Hebrides may be observed today in the numerous ruins of castles and in a diverse and widespread collection of ecclesiastical antiquities, most particularly churches, chapels, grave slabs and Celtic crosses. The church at Rodel on Harris is one of the most famous of these sites.

The Donald Lordship was finally broken in 1493 when King James IV forcibly demanded that they forfeit their power, thereby bringing the Isles within the realm of Scotland. The resulting power vacuum in the islands had the effect of strengthening the independence of the individual clans, which in turn led to infighting and centuries of skirmishes among themselves. Every island has its harrowing accounts of clan battles, a violent succession of betrayal, retribution and ruthless massacre.

Clan chiefs built castles as a focal point for their patriarchal systems whereas the clanspeople themselves lived a village lifestyle as pastoralists in single-room dwellings. As blood relatives they were bound together under a common ancestor, vigorously defending clan territories with their lives but always looking to expand upon them and to increase resources. They spoke Gaelic and maintained a mostly Catholic faith in defiance of the Reformation and pressure from the Protestant Lowlands and England. Not until the Jacobite uprising of 1745, however, under the leadership of Charles Edward Stuart (Bonnie Prince Charlie), would the clans finally rally in force more or less under one flag. Jacobite hopes were extinguished, however, with the final disastrous showdown at Culloden in 1746. The Highlanders were considerably outnumbered by the Duke of Cumberland's well-armed troops and were decimated in a short battle, effectively finishing off the clan system for ever. Clan chiefs thereafter were forbidden their own armies and many Hebridean clans lost their land in the process.

In the second half of the eighteenth century, the population of the Hebrides increased dramatically. The potato replaced barley and oats as the main crop and the system of crofting developed. Crofting is a unique form of small-scale land use, with individual family-run units of about five to ten acres. The practice of creating lazy-beds was widespread in the eighteenth and nineteenth centuries, where poor, shallow acid soil was laboriously cultivated to create depth and fertility by adding seaweed and animal dung. Evidence of these lazy-beds can be seen today in the furrowed ridges that have scarred the rough moorland areas on many islands, on patches close to where crofting communities settled in townships. Fishing, grazing and kelp harvesting supplemented the growing of crops, although fishing was only properly developed as an industry in the nineteenth century. The indigenous croft houses of the time were known as **blackhouses** on Harris and Lewis, while traditional houses on islands farther to the south were simply referred to as **thatched houses**. With thick walls and a thatched roof for insulation, the blackhouse was built narrow, low and streamlined to deflect the wind. On Lewis, there is a Blackhouse Museum at Arnol, and at Gearranan there is a restored village of half a dozen or so of this type of housing.

As in the Highlands, the people of the Hebrides suffered great hardship and upheaval during the notorious Highland Clearances of the nineteenth century. Only Colonsay and one or two other places escaped its disastrous consequences, a tragedy exacerbated by the potato famine of 1845. People were often forcibly evicted from their homes and dispossessed of the land from which they eked a living to make way for more profitable sheep and to establish deer estates. It is perhaps not surprising that such tragedy was destined to take place, in a land populated by subsistence communities at the mercy and eventual betrayal of the recently installed capitalistic 'lairds'. In many cases, the new landlords were the old clan chiefs. It seems rather a sad irony that the old clan chiefs became the new tyrants, having learned nothing, it seemed, from their own oppression in the centuries before. But there was also another more insidious agenda to the clearances, beyond a greedy few selling out to market economics. The overriding ambition of the conspiracy was, undoubtedly, the extinction of the Gaelic population.

The Hebridean landscape is today littered with numerous **abandoned townships**. There are many opportunities for visitors to stroll among the sad ruins of crumbling cottages, amid silences that would once have been filled by sounds of toil, banter, despair, laughter and music. Nothing, it seems, can entirely dispel the melancholy that, like the creeping ivy and deep-rooted moss, now clings to the empty window ledges and cold hearths. The final insult perhaps is that they are now little more than toilets for those innocent vehicles of the displacement that has taken place: blackface sheep.

The fishing industry is today also a shadow of what it was and continues to decline because of overfishing. Similarly, the desertification of Scotland will never be reversed as long as there are so many sheep and deer. Reduction in their numbers and peopled again, the land would likely be the better for it – better worked, richer in wildlife and habitat and more beautiful to the eye because a kind of balance would have been restored.

Despite the depopulation, crofting remains one of the principal economic activities of the Hebrides in the twenty-first century. However, fishing, fish farming, quarrying, tourism and the service sector are equally important. Today's crofters normally have second jobs in other areas. Fish farming is a major employer, although the incongruous sight of salmon cages in almost every sea loch, as well as their environmental impact, is a contentious issue. Such activities are in conflict with what is the region's major asset, its scenery. The small-scale manufacture of Harris Tweed cloth and various craft products is also important in certain localities. Other islands where hill farming is a primary activity are confronting the prospect of a second clearance, driven this time not by the profitability of sheep but quite the opposite. Sheep farming is in crisis because ewes are fetching their lowest prices for decades, brought about by various crises, including foot and mouth disease in 2001.

Many communities in the Hebrides have lived with depopulation for years, primarily because there are no viable employment prospects. Social and financial imperatives are generally lacking, so there is little incentive for young people and families to stay. Old buildings are, on some of the more popular islands, undergoing renovation and finding a new lease of life as holiday homes for people from the mainland. Other incomers are moving to the islands in search of the 'good life'. The unfairness of the property market is such that native Hebrideans are often forced to live in new, cheaper, incongruous bungalows. But it is a resourceful and defiant people that remains in the Hebrides, clinging on to a far-from-easy way of life and yet retaining a distinct identity and an indomitable pride.

Celtic Culture and the Gaelic Language

'Music and song, laddie, you must have that in you, or the island will lose its soul.'
Angus MacKinnon, twelfth-generation islander of Eigg, during the
campaign for the community buyout of Eigg in 1997.

The origin of the term 'Celtic' is thought to be Greek. The ancient Greeks first used it to describe 'the barbaric peoples' of central and west-central Europe, the *Keltoi*. Prompted by Roman invasions, the Celts began spreading from continental Europe to Britain during the fifth century BC. As well as introducing new skills in working iron they also brought with them their dialects of the Celtic tongue. The first Celts in the Hebrides are thought to have arrived a century or so later.

The early Celtic tribes had a great passion for war, despite having established a predominantly matriarchal society. Women were, according to a Greek witness, 'not only equal to their husbands in stature, but they rival them in strength as well'. The Celts fashioned effective weapons and tools in metal and the chieftains developed a fondness for gold ornaments. For most ordinary folk in the islands at this time, however, the basis of individual wealth was dependent on the size of flocks and herds.

The modern definition of Celtic people is, to a large extent, based on a common language root, but there may still exist distinct differences, such as between the Welsh and the Gaelic tongues. Throughout history, wherever they have settled in Europe, the Celts have also shown a distinct uniformity with regard to ornament, burial mode, ritual and belief. In pre-Christian times, the worship of innumerable Celtic gods and goddesses was perpetuated by the druids. Contrary to New Age myths, however, this ancient priesthood had no association whatsoever with rituals at much earlier archaeological sites, such as stone circles. In pagan Celtic mythology, animals such as the boar and stag were held in divine esteem: the boar personified courage and strength among Celtic warriors.

In tandem with the arrival of Christianity, the Gaelic language spread from Ireland in the fifth century. These Irish settlers arrived in Argyll, a regional name that derives from *Arag haidal*, meaning 'Boundary of the Gaels'. They quickly spread, but up until that time, the tongue of the Hebrides was probably a Pictish language.

Four Celtic languages survive today: Breton, Welsh, Irish Gaelic and Scottish Gaelic. Scottish Gaelic, although still with its linguistic root in the Irish version, has evolved into a separate tongue. Gaelic remains a living language among roughly 50,000 speakers, with its stronghold in northwest Scotland, including the Western Isles, on Skye and in a few other places in the Hebrides. Gaelic is a complex tongue with an alphabet of only eighteen letters and an antiquated grammar. Recent years have seen a dramatic rise in the number of Gaelic language learners, and not only in the islands. This renaissance has spread beyond spoken Gaelic to Gaelic literature and music as well as a more general interest in Celtic cultural activities. Most names for places and landscape features that appear on Ordnance Survey maps of the Hebrides are, though frequently misspelt, of Gaelic origin. In the Western Isles there is also a strong Norse influence. **Appendix 1** has a glossary of Gaelic terms. Road signs in the Hebrides are normally in both English and Gaelic.

The first Celtic church in the islands was the sixth-century monastery at Iona, which successfully distanced itself from Roman Catholicism and remained the national church of Scotland for 150 years. As well as being a religious sanctuary, Iona became a centre for craftsmanship. Scattered throughout the Hebrides can be found a number of particularly fine examples of Celtic crosses, many carved and engraved by the gifted stone masons on Iona.

At the community level, the Gaelic-speaking islands now host a number of arts festival (*Feisean*) every year in celebration of Celtic art, from painting to drama and traditional singing to the bagpipes, accordion and clarsach (small harp). Fèis Bharraigh (the Barra Community Arts Festival) was the first and has taken place each July since 1981. It has led to a phenomenally successful movement that has spread beyond the islands to the mainland and prompted Michael Russell MSP to say, 'The Fèis movement has done more to revitalise Gaelic society than a hundred Civil Service studies . . .' Music and dancing predominate, including Scottish folk dancing as well as rare displays of unique Hebridean dancing, a highly individual storytelling form of dance. Emotive songs of exile are a recurring theme in Gaelic singing while storytelling is also an important part of the collective folk memory of the islands. Legends, folklore and anecdotes can pass on through many generations of a community's unwritten history.

What has been written down might be expressed in any one of the forms of literature, from poetry and prose to fiction and non-fiction. Many of Scotland's foremost contemporary writers live on or have connections with islands: writers such as John Murray, Finlay MacLeod, Iain Crichton Smith and

Donald MacAulay, most of whom write or wrote in their native Gaelic as well as English. A fine library of Gaelic literature exists at Canna House, on the island of Canna.

As with the Highlanders, common blood lines and clan kinship continue to be powerful bonds between islanders. For centuries, clan territories have been associated with particular areas: the MacNeils in Barra, the MacDonalds in Eigg and the Uists, the MacLeods in Skye and Harris, and the Mackinnons in Mull. Even after the Protestant Reformation in Scotland, the Highlands and Islands were a bastion of Catholicism, the clans later rallying to the Jacobite cause under Bonnie Prince Charlie. Their defeat led to the dominance of a number of Presbyterian religious beliefs in the Hebrides. During the clearances, the missionaries of the Free Church seized the opportunity to increase their flock by offering false hope to the dispossessed. Barra, South Uist and Eigg are among a handful of islands to have remained largely Roman Catholic.

Many of the islands have established their own historical societies, with the larger more populated places such as Stornoway having arts centres and museums as well. Each in its own way is dedicated to promoting a local Gaelic heritage through a greater understanding of the past. From a unique resource, visitors thus have the opportunity to appreciate a particular island perspective on history. It is unlikely you will have to wait too long before getting involved in island life yourself, while having fun at the same time, when the invitation comes to attend a *ceilidh*. On the smaller islands, these are normally held in the community hall, where the whole island turns up for a long evening of live music, country dancing and drinking. Hebrideans are used to making their own entertainment, partly out of necessity, partly out of a simple love of life. In many places, *ceilidhs* are the main social events and can crop up at any time of the year, sometimes spontaneously. The best are usually at Hogmanay or when celebrating something special such as Eigg Independence Day, on 12 June.

For a multitude of reasons, depopulation continues throughout the Hebrides. Nevertheless, community confidence in a common heritage, a resurgence of interest in a common language and a pride in a unique cultural identity show no sign of waning.

CHAPTER 7

The Islands and The Walks

Eigg

On 12 June 1997, the residents of Eigg, in partnership with Highland Council and the Scottish Wildlife Trust, secured a landmark victory. After a long-running appeal, aided by high-profile media attention, the Isle of Eigg Heritage Trust achieved the nearest thing to independence the Hebrides has seen in any living islander's memory. After years of neglect by previous owners, social justice, environmental welfare and long-term prosperity are now, perhaps for the first time, top of the agenda on Eigg. Time will be the judge of the ultimate success of the Trust's endeavours. Its motto is 'Cuir dochas air an Eilean' ('giving hope to the island'), and in the years since the historic community buyout a number of improvements have already taken shape. The great hope for the twenty-first century will be that Eigg might show the way and encourage other Highland and island communities to overturn the rule of mismanagement that can result from absentee landlordship. By 2002, Gigha had taken the same, bold step.

Eigg is the historic capital of the parish known as the Small Isles, the island group immediately to the south of Skye that also includes Muck, Rum and Canna. Of the four, it has the greatest population and is the second largest island in area after Rum. Scenically, it is the most varied, with a corresponding diversity of wildlife habitats. As a result of SWT's part in the Isle of Eigg Heritage Trust, many areas of the island are now being managed and extended for the long-term benefit of flora and fauna and to increase the biodiversity still further. From April to September, the SWT warden organises guided walks for visitors.

The island has unique geological features, the most striking of which is the remarkable wedge of pitchstone rock known as **An Sgurr** (Walk 1). At the **Bay of Laig** (Walk 2) can be found the finest beach in the Small Isles. There are also fascinating aspects of the island's history to seek out, a saga of human occupation that stretches back some 8,000 years but which in the last 1,000 years is marked by a succession of particularly tragic and bloody events. Episodes of savage retribution have frequently laid the island to waste, and famine and neglect have led to great suffering. In his book *The Cruise of the Betsey*, Hugh Miller commented on the extreme poverty of 1840s' Eigg: 'I saw her husband a few days after – an old worn-out man, with famine written legibly in his hollow cheek and eye. . . . They had no means of living, he said, save through the charity of their poor neighbours, who had so little to spare; for the parish or the proprietor had never given them anything.'

For its size, there is a good deal to see and do on Eigg. There is one cave that remembers the suffocating cries of a massacred population and another that has heard the silent preachings of a forbidden congregation; there are birds and flowers, and, of course, there are sands that sing.

MAIN SETTLEMENTS

Eigg has 70 inhabitants, the greater proportion of whom live in Cleadale, in the northern part of the island around the Bay of Laig. Cleadale is about 5.5 km/3^1/$_2$ mi north along the island road from Galmisdale, which has the pier. Galmisdale also houses the main facilities, including shop, post office, tearoom, toilets and petrol pump. There is also a craft shop by the pier, the best source of further information on the island.

ACCESS

The Cal Mac passenger ferry *Lochnevis* operates from Mallaig four or five times a week. This vessel also serves Rum, Muck and Canna. The MV *Shearwater* (telephone 01687 450224) operates from Arisaig six days per week between May and September (including Sundays; no service on Thursdays), less frequently out of season. Because of unsuitable conditions for landing at Galmisdale pier, passengers are transferred between the ferry and the island by a small launch.

ACCOMMODATION

B&B accommodation is limited. Try Sue or Kay Kirk at Laig Farm (telephone 01687 482 405). Lageorna is a self-catering house sleeping up to six people (telephone as above). The Glebe Barn bunkhouse (Simon or Karen Helliwell, telephone 01687 482417) opened 1999, greatly assisting the accommodation shortage on Eigg. It can accommodate up to 24, and I highly recommend it. It is one of the best equipped and most comfortable of its kind, with fabulous views across the sea to Lochaber. There are also two very basic bothies available (telephone 01687 482486) in other parts of the island.

PUBLIC TRANSPORT

A minibus service operates from Galmisdale pier to Cleadale and the Singing Sands, corresponding with ferry times. Apart from transporting you and your luggage, motorised transport is not necessary for moving around the island. Cycling, however, is an option, and bicycles may be hired at the pier.

ORDNANCE SURVEY LANDRANGER MAPS
Landranger sheet 39 covers Eigg and all the Small Isles group.

MAIN PLACES OF INTEREST
An Sgurr (1) Walk 1
Bay of Laig (2) Walk 2
Beinn Bhuidhe (3) Walk 2
Camas Sgiotaig or 'Singing Sands' (4) Walk 2
Cathedral Cave (MacDonald's Cave) (5) Short Walk 1
Eilean Thuilm (6) Northern tip of Eigg where fossilised fish and reptiles might be found
Fossilised tree (7) To be seen at the foot of the rampart of An Sgurr
Grulin (8) Walk 1
Kildonnan Chapel (11) Short Walk 2
Kildonnan Cross (12) Short Walk 2
Lodge (9) Short Walk 2
Massacre Cave (St Francis Cave) (10) Short Walk 1

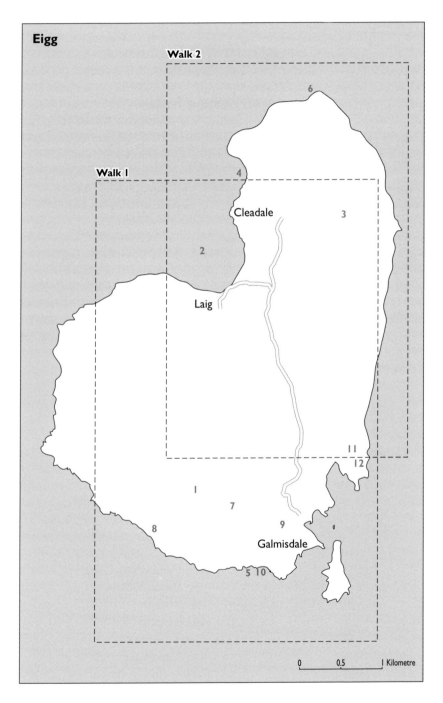

Eigg

Walk 2

Walk 1

6

4

Cleadale

3

2

Laig

11

12

1

7

9

8

Galmisdale

5 10

0   0.5   I Kilometre

WALK 1

An Sgurr and Grulin

Main interest and sights	A unique summit experience, the sad but beautiful ruins of a pre-clearance township and wildlife; An Sgurr (1) Grulin (8)
Route	Circular
Grade	Moderate/strenuous
Map	OS Landranger sheet 39
Starting point	Galmisdale, GR 484839
Finishing point	As above
Distance	9.5 km/6 mi ($4^1/_4$ hours)
Paths and terrain	Clearly marked paths with short sharp climb to rocky summit ridge. Unpathed and steep descent to Grulin
Options	(a) If uncertain of your navigational abilities, it is best to return from the summit of An Sgurr in reverse of the upward route (moderate, $3^1/_2$ hours) (b) Beinn Tighe – from An Sgurr, head northwards to Beinn Tighe via Loch nam Ban Móra and Loch Beinn Tighe. Return south to regain the main route (moderate/strenuous, 6 hours) (c) It is easy to integrate Short Walk 2 into the return from Grulin
Nearby walks	Short Walks 1, 2 and 3
Refreshments	Galmisdale Post Office shop and tearoom by the pier

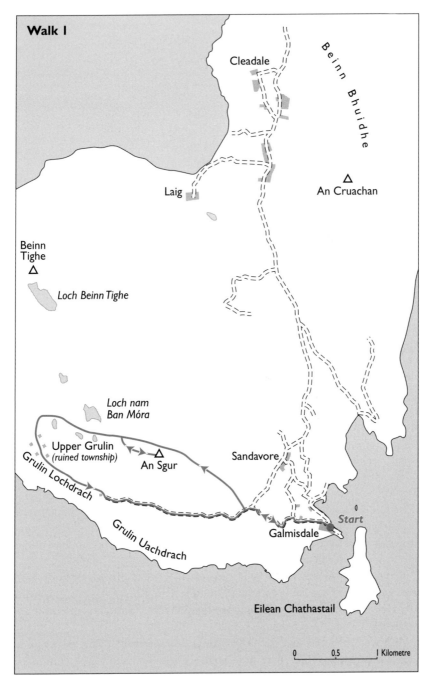

Walk 1

Cleadale

Beinn Bhuidhe

An Cruachan △

Laig

Beinn Tighe △

Loch Beinn Tighe

Loch nam Ban Móra

Upper Grulin (ruined township)

An Sgur △

Sandavore

Grulin Lochdrach

Grulin Uachdrach

Start

Galmisdale

Eilean Chathastail

0   0.5   1 Kilometre

The 52-million-year-old volcanic monolith known as **An Sgurr** (1) is one of the most distinctive landmarks in the Hebrides. Nowhere else is there anything quite like the sight of this great wedge of columnar pitchstone rock (solidified lava that cooled quickly) rising abruptly in isolation and entirely dominating the island. There is also nothing to equal the feeling of exuberance when standing at the vertiginous extremity of its eastern prow. The return from the summit is via pre-clearance township ruins situated above a beautiful coastline. Eigg is also renowned for its proliferation and diversity of flowering plants and bird life, and the environs of An Sgurr are as rewarding in this respect as other parts of the island.

Leave Galmisdale by the track going west from the pier. Pass to the right of the 'Independence Stone', overlooking the bay and commemorating 12 June 1997. Walk along the edge of the woodland in the vicinity of the Lodge (Short Walk 2). There is much of botanical interest among the trees including, in summer, the delicate enchanter's nightshade. From the top of the wood the bold upthrust of An Sgurr is an arresting sight.

When above the trees, continue to the cottage to join the track running southwest from Sandavore. Turn left, then after 100 m bear right at a cairn for a path rising over the moorland, towards An Sgurr. Skirt below the north side of this dramatic wall of solid rock, the one chink in its seeming impregnable armour encountered roughly 400 m/¼ mi before Loch nam Ban Móra. On curving in to the left, almost immediately trend farther left to climb a steep slope leading up to a crumbling drystone wall and a cairn on the main massif. Walk another 600 m/³⁄₈ mi to reach the summit (1¾ hours), which is at the far eastern extremity of the ridge. This direct route across the rocky crest has few obstacles and is a marvellously airy experience with superb views to Skye, Rum, Canna and Muck. A less unnerving option is possible, however, along a slightly lower path on the right.

Try standing at the very end of the ridge directly above the eastern prow and just a few metres beyond the summit. It is a powerful feeling, an experience not to disappoint those who have ever fantasised about holding command of some great sailing ship. Perhaps it gives an insight into how Viking seafarers must have felt a thousand years ago, riding high over the seas of the Hebrides, master mariners of the northern oceans.

Return to the base of the pitchstone massif, just southeast of Loch nam Ban Móra. The next 1.5 km/1 mi of the walk, between An Sgurr and **Grulin** (8), is over unpathed and largely untrodden territory but offers the most interesting continuation of the descent.

Aim west to skirt above the north sides of three small lochans, passing one after the other, each in its own little hollow. From the last of them, continue a a further 100 m west and then turn south and head down a steep slope. Make a beeline for the now visible crumbling outlines of what were once the cottages of Upper Grulin, cleared in 1853 and no longer marked on OS Landranger maps. From here, follow a well-trodden path all the way back to Galmisdale. With the rugged dark-grey ramparts of An Sgurr rising dramatically on one side and the little island of Muck, across the Sound of Eigg, on the other, this homeward coastal stretch is an absolute delight on a summer's evening.

The Sgurr, Eigg

Laig and the Singing Sands

Main interest and sights	The special phenomenon of Singing Sands and fantastic views to Rum: Bay of Laig (2) Camas Sgiotaig (Singing Sands) (4) Beinn Bhuidhe (3)
Route	Circular
Grade	Easy/moderate
Map	OS Landranger sheet 39
Starting point	Main island road just south of Cleadale, GR 477873
Finishing point	As above
Distance	7.2 km/4^{1}/$_{2}$ mi (3 hours)
Paths and terrain	Mostly clearly marked paths and a road, with little gradient
Options	Energetic hill-walkers should include an ascent of the moorland plateau of Beinn Bhuide. From the Singing Sands, climb the steep east ridge by a zigzag path up grass to the summit of Dùn an Thalasgair. Stay close to the edge of the basalt escarpment, going south to An Cruachan, descending southwest from there to the road (moderate/strenuous, 4^{1}/$_{4}$ hours)
Nearby walks	Short Walk 3
Refreshments	None en route; nearest at Galmisdale – post office shop and tearoom by the pier

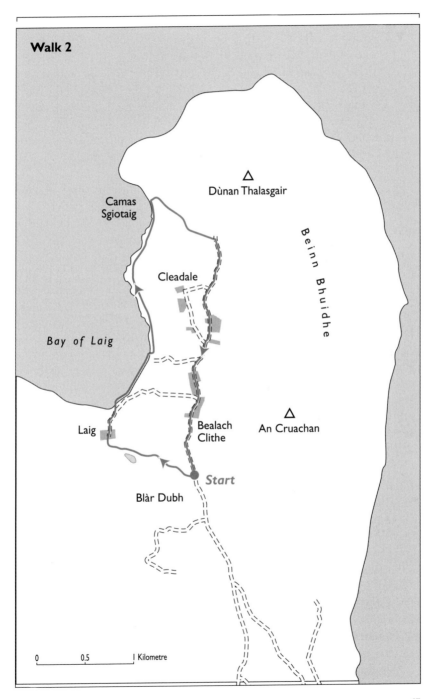

Walk 2

Dùnan Thalasgair △

Camas Sgiotaig

Beinn Bhuidhe

Cleadale

Bay of Laig

Bealach Clithe

An Cruachan △

Laig

Start

Blàr Dubh

0   0.5   1 Kilometre

More than one Hebridean island claims to have a beach where the sands are said to sing. It is perhaps not surprising, therefore to discover that Eigg is one of these, but the sands at **Camas Sgiotaig** (4) are in fact very worthy of the description 'Singing Sands'. Just south of here, also within close vicinity of Cleadale, is the longest and probably the finest beach in the Small Isles. On this walk you will explore and enjoy throughout the walk coastal fringes that are gently sloping and golden, croft lands that are fertile and green, and exposures of rock that are rugged and dark, all against a backdrop of the Rum hills, one of the most awesome mountainous profiles in the islands.

Just south of Cleadale, about 1 km/²/₃ mi north of the post office, seek out a muddy path beginning among scrub on the west side of the road. It is not too easy to find, but look for a little footbridge over a burn located farther below. Depending on where you are staying on the island, you will either have to walk to this starting point, catch the island taxi (white Transit van) or begin the walk from your accommodation in Cleadale.

Drop down the slope, go over the footbridge and follow a path to the right, somewhat overgrown in places. Having crossed a ditch, the path leads up to a point above an impressive gorge with a waterfall. Be careful here of the sharp drop on your right. This is a fantastic viewpoint over the northwest corner of Eigg, across the **Bay of Laig** (2) and to the dramatic profile of the Cuillin of Rum. The extensive escarpment of **Beinn Bhuide** (3) consists of a 2.5 km/ 1¹/₂ mi-long basaltic wall, 100 m/330 ft-high cliffs running north to south behind Cleadale. Although expressed here on a smaller scale, comparisons with Totternish on Skye (Walks 9 and 10) spring to mind.

Go over a low fence and then drop down to the farm at Laig. Cross a stream and gain a track leading to the back of the beach. Immediately to the right of where the river draining Gleann Chàradail enters the sea, go over a stile to reach the beach. Walk across the sands at the Bay of Laig, the island's finest beach, to reach the north side. From here, continue north above low, pale sandstone cliffs to reach the famous Singing Sands Bay at Camas Sgiotaig (1¹/₂ hours). If you test the claim, you will find, sure enough, that the sands do squeak and squeal in an unusual way when trodden upon. Musical associations, however, seem somewhat exaggerated, but nevertheless Camas Sgiotaig provides a most convincing example of Singing Sands. The songs that resonate on this beach are a frictional phenomenon, the sound of thousands of tiny grains of quartz moving against each other when pressure is applied. Take a closer look also at the surrounding sandstone cliffs, where erosion has resulted in some unusual rock formations.

Walk up from the beach and aim for the white house at Howlin, at the northern extremity of Cleadale. Notice to your right a large reed bed and wetland area. Sedge warblers are frequently seen and heard here, and there are many wild flowers on the marsh.

At the aforementioned house, join a track that leads on to the tarmac road for Cleadale and the southern half of the island. Continue past the bungalows and cottages strung out in a line parallel to the spectacular curtain of rock and buttress behind. If you are self-catering, make a point of stopping at a bungalow on the left in Cleadale, selling the biggest and tastiest eggs on Eigg: fresh duck eggs 'Hot from the Bot', as a prominent sign on the road advertises them.

Short Walks

I THE CAVES (I³/₄ HOURS; OSLR MAP 39)

This walk explores two remarkable coastal caves with, as you might well have come to expect in this part of the world, a tragic history.

Walk west from the pier at Galmisdale, passing 'Independence Stone' on the right and following the track through the wood. After about 10 minutes, go through a gate on the left, along a path skirting the southwestern edge of the woodland. Beyond a burn, pass to the left of a bungalow and bear west again below an obvious outcrop. Go over the sheep fencing to find a path at the mouth of a burn that descends steeply to the shore.

Cathedral Cave (5) (MacDonald's Cave, GR 472834) is 300 m west along the rocky beach. It is a huge cave, imbued with the silent air of melancholy entirely befitting its status as a sanctuary for prayer. It is still occasionally used for Catholic services, a custom originating from eighteenth-century persecutions when the people of Eigg were forced, literally, to go under-ground with their faith.

Massacre Cave (10) (St Francis Cave, GR 476834) is about 150 m south-east of the end of the path, over the sometimes treacherous rocks and ledges along the shore in the other direction. It is best not to attempt this at high tide. In this cave, in the winter of 1577, the MacLeods from Skye trapped 395 MacDonalds, men, women and children, and suffocated them all by setting fire to brushwood at the entrances, thus wiping out the entire population of Eigg. This 'dreadful work of indiscriminate vengeance', as Walter Scott later described it, was in revenge for the castration of some of the MacLeod men by the MacDonalds, an act in itself retribution for the raping of MacDonald girls. Disputes between the two clans had a long and bitter history.

Return the same way before the tide comes in.

2 THE LODGE GROUNDS (I¹/₂ HOURS; OSLR MAP 39)

This walk explores the luxuriant grounds of the old **Lodge** (9), built in the 1920s by the laird, Lord Runciman.

Follow the track west from Galmisdale pier, as for Walk 1 and Short Walk 1. Turn right just beyond a pink house in the trees. Eigg Community Hall is on the left, venue for some of the best ceilidhs in the Hebrides, especially each 12 June. The Lodge gardens begin here, at an old orchard. When in season, rhododendrons, fuchsia and roses bring about a blaze of colour. Prompted by the mild, damp air of the Gulf Stream, palm trees also flourish, accentuating the Mediterranean aspect of the Italianate Lodge building. With its lawns and lush gardens sheltered from relentless Hebridean gales by trees on all sides, the Lodge gardens are a leafy retreat.

There is little to see inside the Lodge, which is normally locked anyway, but in the porch at the front door there are two or three interesting Celtic cross-slabs. These relics were pillaged by previous owners from various ecclesiastical sites in other parts of the island.

Continue north from the Lodge and go along a track to meet the road at a letterbox. Turn right and walk back down to Galmisdale.

3 GALMISDALE AND KILDONNAN (2¹/₄ HOURS; OSLR MAP 39)

The best of the island's woodlands are to be found on the slopes immediately above Galmisdale Bay. Farther to the north, on the north side of Kildonnan Bay, lie the interesting ruins of a church and an ancient Celtic cross-slab. Along the coast in between, tidal flats occupy two large and beautiful bays from which there are outstanding views to the mainland.

From the pier, follow the island road around Galmisdale Bay to where the road turns uphill. Instead of walking along the road, continue around the bay on a track. Just before a burn at the north end of the bay, GR 484843, strike off up towards the top end of a grassy woodland glade. From here a path continues beside a burn through lovely hazel scrub and other trees, leading eventually to the road again.

Follow the road north past a church on the left, worth a quick visit to view its attractive timber interior or simply to take in the sedate atmosphere for a while. Just beyond a standing stone on the right, cut across the rough ground as a short cut for reaching the road to Kildonnan. Walk down the road towards the sea, but at a cattle grid turn sharp left off the tarmac for a track that curves round to the site of the ruined **Kildonnan Chapel** (11) and **Kildonnan Cross** (12). Within the walls of the fifteenth-century chapel, grave slabs are becoming obscured by an encroaching carpet of vegetation. Outside the ruins stands the Celtic cross, although the top third has now broken off and is lying flat. The views across the bay to the Lochaber mountains are exceptionally fine from here. To get on to the sands at Kildonnan, walk down to the last house.

Low tide, when the tidal flats are exposed, is the best time to walk around the bay to reach the rocks at the south end. Oystercatchers nest on the thrift-carpeted skerries, trained by the Luftwaffe it seems. Cowering and ducking from the dive-bombing birds, follow the shore along to reach Galmisdale Bay and the road.

Rum

Rum is by far the largest of the Small Isles, an island now given over entirely to nature. It is owned and managed as a National Nature Reserve (NNR) by Scottish Natural Heritage (SNH), having been declared a Biosphere Reserve in 1957. Visiting Rum has its logistical problems, but these should not deter you.

Perhaps the best-known association of Rum with wildlife are with sea eagles, Rum ponies and Manx shearwaters. Having been shot and poisoned to extinction by the beginning of the twentieth century, the white-tailed sea eagle was reintroduced to Rum in 1975, using Norwegian birds. It is now successfully extending its range along the west coast of Scotland. Rum ponies are a unique breed, small in stature and deriving from crossbred Highland and Arab ponies. These animals can be seen grazing the grass around Kinloch Castle while Rum's mountain tops are home to the world's largest breeding colony of Manx shearwaters. Over 100,000 of the birds return to the island each spring, having wintered in the Atlantic waters off Brazil. Each night in early summer, the Rum Cuillin is a breathtaking, pulsating theatre of sound and activity as the birds return to their high-level nest burrows after a day at sea, feeding.

Rum has long been an important deer forest, these animals having been hunted by clan chiefs from as early as the Middle Ages. Today, the island is an important deer study area and access to certain northern sectors is frequently restricted because of this. Other parts are currently undergoing a long-term woodland regeneration programme to create a habitat resembling that which existed before Rum was stripped treeless by human beings.

Rum has a couple of architectural oddities in the form of the castle at Kinloch and a mausoleum at Harris, expressions of the extravagant eccentricity of the early twentieth-century owner George Bullough. Ruined townships and antiquities are also to be seen. A Mesolithic beach site above the northwest corner of Loch Scresort provides evidence of the earliest human settlement yet found in Scotland. Radiocarbon dating suggests occupation from about 6500 BC. But above all, Rum is a place for mountain lovers, naturalists and those who relish truly wild landscapes.

The **Cuillin of Rum** (6) is perhaps the island's biggest attraction, a dramatic and challenging range to which a growing number of hill-walkers are drawn. The Cuillin is what remains of an extinct volcano. The Torridonian sandstone cliffs of the west coast add to the immense geological complexity of the island.

Come extremely well prepared if you intend to go walking on Rum. Rainfall is typically frequent, heavy and prolonged, and wherever you choose to wander on the island, rough walking on arduous terrain is guaranteed. Be aware, also, that a summer's day on Rum has transformed many a peaceful nature lover into a serial killer. SNH's encouragement of wildlife seems to have aided and abetted the midge population. Exterminating Rum's man-eating midges is a battle you are certain to lose without copious quantities of repellent in your armoury. Midge nets are the bestselling item in the island shop.

MAIN SETTLEMENTS

All thirty inhabitants of Rum live at Kinloch, at the head of Loch Scresort. Most of the population are SNH workers and their families, but in an attempt to address concern about the lack of other employment and business opportunities, SNH is soon intending to release for sale land around the village. At Kinloch there is a primary school, a post office shop and the small ferry pier. The bistro at Kinloch Castle is the only place to eat out although a teashop at the Community Hall opens in summer, at times to coincide with the arrival of day visitors. Trail guides and information on wildlife are available from the Reserve Office.

The Old Pier, Rum

ACCESS

The Cal Mac passenger ferry *Lochnevis*, which serves the Small Isles from Mallaig, calls at Rum four times a week. There is a short transfer journey to the pier by the island boat *Rhouma*. MV *Shearwater* (telephone 01687 450224) from Arisaig sails to Rum three days per week from May to September; two days per week out of season.

ACCOMMODATION

Kinloch Castle hostel (£11 pp per night, telephone 01687 462037) is the only 'comfortable' accommodation for visitors staying overnight. With single, double, twin and shared rooms in the old servants' quarters, it is more like a simple hotel, with the bistro on-site. There are also four bothies providing basic self-catering accommodation in the village, each equipped with fuel, beds and mattresses. Two very basic mountain bothies are to be found on the island, in Glen Dibidil and at Guirdil. All accommodation on Rum must be booked in advance.

PUBLIC TRANSPORT

There are no tarmacked roads on Rum, only a rough track through Kinloch Glen, with branches off to Kilmory and to Harris. They are suitable only for SNH Landrovers, although mountain bikes may be brought over and used on these tracks. For everyone else wishing to get to other parts of the islands beyond Kinloch, it is necessary to walk. Those staying at the castle will have their baggage transferred from the pier by the warden.

ORDNANCE SURVEY LANDRANGER MAPS

Landranger sheet 39 covers Rum and all the Small Isles group.

MAIN PLACES OF INTEREST

Askival (1) Walk 3 (Options)
Bagh na h-Uamba (2) Short Walk 4
Barkeval (3) Walk 3
Bloodstone Hill (4) Walk 4 (Options)
Bullough Mausoleum (5) Walk 4
Cuillin of Rum (6) See page 52 and Walk 3 and Walk 4
Glen Dibidil (7) A dramatic situation, surrounded by a horseshoe of Cuillin peaks
Hallival (8) Walk 3 (Options)
Harris Bay (9) Walk 4
Kilmory (10) Walk 4 (Options)

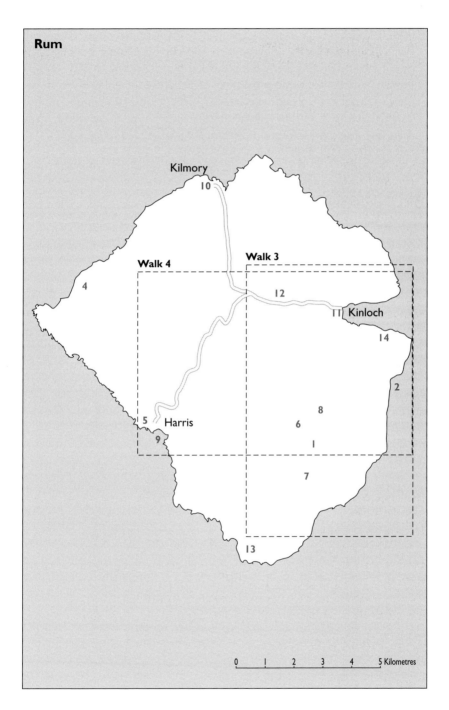

Rum

Kilmory

10

Walk 4

Walk 3

4

12

11 Kinloch

14

2

5

Harris

9

8

6

1

7

13

0   1   2   3   4   5 Kilometres

Kinloch Castle (11) Something completely different and not to be missed. Red (Arran) sandstone castle built in 1902 by Sir George Bullough, the then owner, reflecting his wealth and left by his widow in 1957 as furnished, in extravagant Edwardian style. Highlights of the interior are a Victorian Jacuzzi bath, a huge mechanical orchestrion and a unique photographic archive from turn-of-the-century scenes around the world, many depicting gruesome executions in Asia. Regular guided tours – £3

Kinloch Glen (12) Walk 4 and Short Walk 5

Loch Papadil (13) Remote, requiring effort to reach; delightful tree-fringed setting overlooking the wild coast

Port na Caranean (14) Short Walk 4

Barkeval and the
Cuillin of Rum

Main interest and sights	A wild walk to the edge of a 60-million-year-old volcano: Barkeval (3) Cuillin of Rum (6)
Route	Linear
Grade	Moderate/strenuous
Map	OS Landranger sheet 39
Starting point	Kinloch Castle, GR 402995
Finishing point	As above
Distance	8 km/5 mi (3³/₄ hours)
Paths and terrain	Well-worn, rough path to the Coir Dubh. Steeper climb at the head of the coire and up on to Barkeval
Options	See also page 60 (a) **Hallival** (8) – the northwest ridge of Hallival is gained from the Bealach Bairc-mheall and is difficult terrain but otherwise without major obstacles (strenuous, 5¹/₄ hours) (b) **Askival** (1) – the highest mountain on Rum, best climbed by continuing south from Hallival. The sharp north ridge is tough going with a hard scramble on the Askival Pinnacle, avoidable by bypassing on the left (strenuous, 7¹/₂ hours)
Nearby walks	Walk 4, Short Walk 4 and Short Walk 5
Refreshments	None en route except at Kinloch; small post office shop and bistro at Kinloch Castle

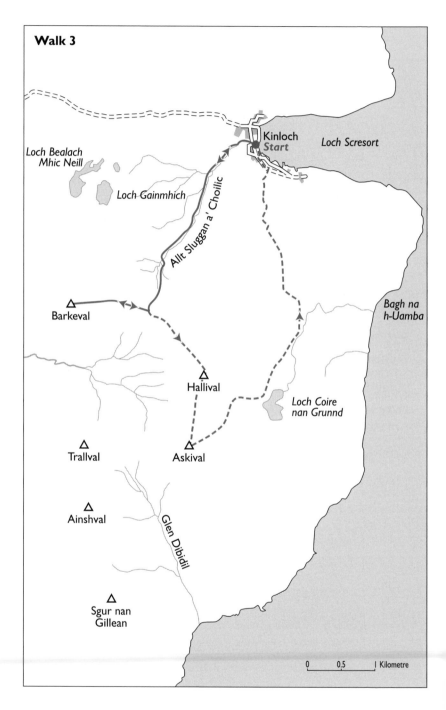

Walk 3

Kinloch
Start

Loch Scresort

Loch Bealach
Mhic Neill

Loch Gainmhich

Allt Sluggan a' Choilic

Bagh na
h-Uamba

△
Barkeval

△
Hallival

Loch Coire
nan Grunnd

△
Trallval

△
Askival

△
Ainshval

Glen Dibidil

△
Sgur nan
Gillean

0   0.5   1 Kilometre

Sixty million years ago, the **Cuillin of Rum** (6) was the core of a huge volcano, a 2 km/1¼ mi-high cone spewing lava over great distances. It would have dominated what would have been then a tropical landscape, before Rum became part of a detached landmass surrounded by sea. These mountain peaks are its visible remains, a rare, layered complex of igneous rocks, revealed thanks to millions of years of erosion. With the exception of the Cuillin of Skye, the Cuillin of Rum boasts the most dramatic peaks in the Hebrides.

Barkeval (3) is at the northern end of the Cuillin, somewhat isolated from the other peaks. It is also the easiest and quickest ascent of any of Rum's principal summits. Just about all walking on Rum, however, is rough and tough, this walk being no exception.

There is no Mountain Rescue team on Rum so, more than anywhere else in Scotland, it is important to fill in a route card and leave the form in the box provided at the SNH office at Kinloch. Begin at Kinloch Castle, on the 'Rum Cuillin' path heading upstream beside the Allt Slugan a' Choilich. A steady ascent traverses a slope newly planted with Scots pine saplings, part of a long-term plan to regenerate the woodlands. Unfortunately, more plants usually mean more insects. Rum midges, renowned for their ferocity, together with clegs that have the size and disposition of vampire bats, have, if anything, further proliferated as a result of SNH's striving for a diverse flora and fauna.

At the top of the replanted area, go through a gate at the deer fence and on to the Coire Dubh. The corrie is frequented by surprisingly tame red deer. Go over a small dam and then walk up the left bank of a burn draining the corrie headwall to reach the Bealach Bairc-mheall, the col between Barkeval and **Hallival** (8). Turn right and ascend the east ridge of Barkeval, the summit being at its western extremity.

Barkeval is said to be the largest mass of peridotite (coarse-grained lava-type rock) in Britain. But the island's rocks are geologically important in many other ways, one of the most noteworthy being that the Rum Cuillin provides a convenient site for studying the internal workings of a volcano. On Barkeval's moonscape summit, one gains the impression of detachment from the higher hills, yet, at the same time, also a sense of being part of something bigger. The feeling is realised on surveying the weathered relics of the old magma core in the form of **Askival** (1) and Trallval, on the opposite side of Atlantic Corrie. Barkeval is also an excellent vantage point from which to scan the wild and empty moorland of the north of the island as well as the scenery beyond its shores, across the sea, to that other spectacular Cuillin on Skye.

The way back to Kinloch is as for the upward route. However, the hill-fit should consider continuing the ridge traverse (see Options), to where summit views become more extensive. When the sun is streaming down on the sea of the Hebrides, the sight of Eigg from Askival is wonderful. But climbing this peak via Hallival has more unusual rewards in store besides. The slopes of both are puckered with the nest burrows of thousands of Manx shearwaters. To see and hear these birds return to their mountain-top nests at midnight, in May and June, is an unforgettable experience. On a sadder note, it is not unusual to come across the occasional Manx carcass. When over the seas, Manx shearwaters are the undisputed masters of acrobatic flight, but they are ill-equipped for moving easily on the ground. This deficiency makes them vulnerable to predation by gulls and crows.

Of further interest to geologists is the remarkable layering of igneous rock seen to good effect on Hallival. This phenomenon was caused by periodic bursts of molten lava spilling on to the surface, each layer cooling before the next pulse arrived.

If you have made it to Askival, descend on its east side via the Coire nan Grunnd, the vicinity of which in June is known to harbour rare fragrant orchids. The complete Cuillin ridge traverse involves taking in also the peaks of Trallval, Ainshival and Sgurr nan Gillean, descending to Glen Dibidil. A classic mountaineering expedition, it is one that requires supreme fitness and the commitment to a very long day.

WALK 4

Harris

Main interest and sights	A coast-to-coast traverse of the island, giving an insight into domestic and agricultural ways in pre-clearance times and a structure dedicated to architectural eccentricity: Kinloch Glen (12) Cuillin of Rum (6) Harris Bay (9) Bullough Mausoleum (5)
Route	Linear
Grade	Moderate/strenuous
Map	OS Landranger sheet 39
Starting point	Kinloch Castle, GR 402995
Finishing point	As above
Distance	21.4 km/13^1/$_4$ mi (6 hours)
Paths and terrain	A long and rough track all the way, involving a 250 m/820 ft ascent and descent in both directions; steepest on the west side
Options	(a) Easily integrated with Short Walk 5 (b) **Kilmory** (10) – From beyond Kinloch Glen, go north on the track through Kilmory Glen. Kilmory has a very fine beach with views to Cuillin of Skye. It once supported a sizeable community; a deserted village and a graveyard remain (moderate, 5^1/$_2$ hours) (c) **Bloodstone Hill** (4) – This third possible route from Kinloch Glen continues west on a path to a hill overlooking the spectacular sea cliffs of Sgorr Mhor (moderate, 6 hours)
Nearby walks	Walk 3, Short Walk 4 and Short Walk 5
Refreshments	None en route except at Kinloch; small post office shop and bistro at Kinloch Castle

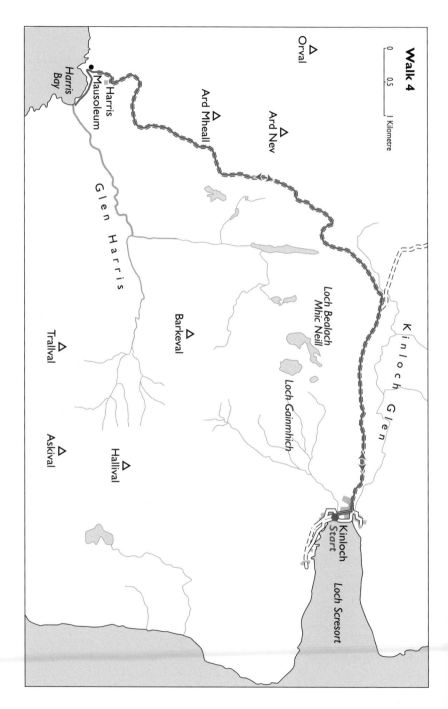

Walk 4

0   0.5   1 Kilometre

Orval

Ard Mheall

Ard Nev

Harris Bay

Harris Mausoleum

Glen Harris

Trallval

Barkeval

Loch Bealach Mhic Neill

Loch Gainmhich

Kinloch Glen

Askival

Hallival

Kinloch Start

Loch Scresort

E vidence of pre-clearance crofting communities on Rum, including associated field systems, is perhaps best seen at Harris, on the west coast. This
walk utilises a long coast-to-coast track, effectively bisecting the island
through the middle and connecting Harris with Kinloch. Apart from the
valuable historical insight into social and domestic life on Rum, awe-inspiring vistas of mountain, ocean and distant landmasses provide unending interest along the way. But the real surprise is the mausoleum at Harris, built in
the incongruous style of a Greek temple.

Leaving Kinloch, follow the track going west by the south side of the
Kinloch River. About 2 km/1^1/$_4$ mi up into **Kinloch Glen** (12), pass the
waterfalls draining Loch Bealach Mhic Neill above the 'Rocking Stone'. The
track forks after a farther 1 km/^{2}/$_3$ mi, the one on the right leading down to
Kilmory (10). Go left instead.

In the vicinity of Long Loch, notice the remains of a failed dam scheme,
'Salisbury's Dam', an overambitious project initiated by the second Marquis
of Salisbury to try to improve salmon fishing in the Kinloch River. The distinctive layered volcanic rocks of the **Cuillin of Rum** (6) can be seen on the
left. From this track, their bold mountain peaks are an endless source of fasci-
nation and wonder, with an especially fine view across Loch an Dornabac.
Before that point, at Malcolm's Bridge (GR 359994), a path on the right de-
parts towards **Bloodstone Hill** (4) but walk on and then down in a steady
descent to **Harris Bay** (9) (2^1/$_2$ hours). Included in the magnificent seaward
panorama are the islands of Mull and Coll, on the southern horizon.

Harris Lodge is near the end of the track at Harris Bay. It was formerly
used by stalkers and their ghillies, but its new role is as a bothy for SNH staff.
The Greek-style **Bullough Mausoleum** (5) is close by, fitting awkwardly
into its most un-Mediterranenan-like surroundings perhaps yet undoubtedly
interesting for its indulgent quirkiness. Within its twenty columns the building contains the tombs of John, George and Monica Bullough.

Above the bay can be found the remains of about thirty houses and barns
abandoned by a crofting community. There is evidence of an extensive lazy-
bed system in the vicinity of the Glen Duian burn, and the fertile soil of
Harris enabled an arable system to be established here more easily than elsewhere on Rum. In addition, the bay enjoys a significantly drier climate than
the east side of the island.

What has been discovered at Harris provides a fascinating insight into
crofting life. The inhabitants of the township would have kept black Highland cattle as well as goats and a few native sheep for mutton, wool, cheese
and butter. Some fishing would have been practised and, in summer, Manx
shearwaters were eaten. Rum ponies, which are still seen today and are con-

sidered a particularly beautiful breed, would have been used as work animals.

The beach at Harris is of rocks and stones, and among other natural features there is a raised beach. Beware, however, of expending too much more energy here as the return to Kinloch is, as the outward route, long and quite arduous.

The Bullough Mausoleum, Rum

Short Walks

4 PORT NA CARANEAN (1 ³/₄ HOURS; OSLR MAP 39)

For twenty years during the mid-nineteenth century **Port na Caranean** (14) (GR 424988) was a major settlement on Rum, inhabited mainly by immigrants from Skye. Today, a lifeless hush pervades these bracken-smothered ruins overlooking the south shore of Loch Scresort, a silence interrupted in the summer by nesting gulls. This walk follows a well-established path that passes through woodland, dips down to the shore and then rises over heath.

From the school at Kinloch, gain a path where a black arrow points you eastwards. Having crossed an area of mature heather, enter a woodland copse. Here lie the ruins of cottages covered by a thick green skin of mosses and ferns. The walls are well preserved, and stone shelves and fireplaces remain intact.

The path is roughest along the next section, where it dips down to the shore briefly before rising again at the headland of Rubha Port na Caranean. A sign makes it clear you have reached the 'End of South Side Trail'. Crumbling walls, windows and doorways of the extensive deserted township now provide nest sites for scores of gulls. To avoid disturbing them, as well as having to machete your way through the bracken beyond, return to Kinloch. In autumn and winter, however, it is possible to proceed to **Bagh na h-Uamba** (2) to investigate a cave and a Celtic cross-marked stone (GR 423974).

5 KINLOCH GLEN (1 ¹/₂ HOURS; OSLR MAP 39)

In April 1997, on a hillside overlooking Kinloch Castle, the millionth tree since work began in 1957 on restoring biological diversity to Rum was planted. During those 40 years, the woodland regeneration scheme has profoundly altered the east side of the island in the vicinity of Loch Scresort as well as in **Kinloch Glen** (12). The work continues today, and this circular walk allows visitors to observe the variety of habitats that are evolving as a result. It follows a recently established nature trail.

From the buildings on the north side of the bridge over the Kinloch River at Kinloch, follow the white arrows westwards through Kinloch Glen. A path skirts the edge of protected mixed woodlands and passes meadows left to pasture and other fields grazed by Highland cattle (including black ones). Rare plants include unusual thistles, orchids growing on the path itself and numerous wetland flowers.

Turn south at the waterfalls of the burn draining Loch Mitchell and return by walking downstream of the Kinloch River, crossing it at a footbridge to gain the glen track (island road) back to Kinloch.

Skye

Strictly speaking, Skye is no longer an island. A 2.4 km/1^1/$_2$ mi long bridge now spans the narrow strait where the ferry once operated, connecting Eilean a'Cheo ('Island of Mist'), the largest of the Inner Hebrides, to the mainland. But well before the bridge opened in 1995, Skye had long enjoyed a reputation as the most popular of all the Scottish islands. Ease of access is part of Skye's appeal, and the splendour of its scenic attractions and the fact that it facilitates tourism so well will ensure that Skye continues to draw the crowds.

With the magnificent Cuillin range, the Isle of Skye boasts the finest mountain scenery in the British Isles. The Cuillin has become a mecca for rock climbers, and the hills are among the toughest of challenges for ambitious walkers and scramblers. For those of us who prefer to remain bipeds when we go walking, the Trotternish peninsula of north Skye has an endless possibility of walking routes around and among the most unusual of rock formations.

Throughout the 1,386 sq km/535 sq mi of Skye, there can hardly be a spot that does have a legend or historical account attached to it, perhaps because so much has been written about Skye that we now need no longer rely on the sadly abandoned tradition of storytelling to recount Skye's precious heritage. Much of this folklore and history is associated with the numerous castles, brochs and other ruins and monuments that can be found scattered far and wide. It is an island as diverse in its social and natural history as it is varied in its landscapes.

MAIN SETTLEMENTS

Portree (31), strung out around a bay on the east coast, is the attractive island capital and the most convenient base from which to explore the island. The town absorbs the summer crowds reasonably well, and this is where you will find shops, banks and the main tourist information office (telephone 01478 612137). Portree has plenty of accommodation as well as most other facilities, and **The Aros Centre** (45) has a cinema.

The village of Broadford is the other main centre of activity and one that may prove a more convenient base for exploring the south end of the island. Armadale, with its well-known castle, is in the far south and is a useful village from which to explore the Sleat peninsula. **Sabhal Mor Ostaig** (37) ('the big Ostaig barn'), a Gaelic college of high reputation, is at nearby Kilbeg. Uig is at the north end of the island and is a good base if you are planning to also take in the Outer Isles.

ACCESS

Heated debate continues over the virtues of the £25-million Skye Bridge. Certainly, the environmental impact of a $1^1/_2$-mile arc of concrete spanning the entrance to Loch Alsh has proved contentious enough. To add insult to injury, the toll charged has been widely condemned as excessive: at £4.70 each way for a car, it is said to be the most expensive bridge in the world to cross. Pedestrians may cross for free. Love it or hate it, Kyle of Lochalsh on the mainland is now just a minute or two from Kyleakin on the island side, and the bridge is the most convenient access point. A more romantic crossing, however, as well as, perhaps, being an act of symbolic defiance, can still be enjoyed by using the tiny ferry operated by R. MacLeod between Kylerhea on Skye and Glenelg on the mainland (six cars at a time and seasonal, telephone 01599 511302).

From the south, the shortest driving route is to Mallaig from where there is a Cal Mac vehicle and passenger ferry crossing to Armadale. From the west, a Cal Mac vehicle and passenger ferry operates between Skye and the Western Isles (summer only), connecting Uig with Lochmaddy on North Uist and Tarbert on Harris. There are also bus services operated by SkyeWays Travel Ltd (daily, including Sunday, and all year) from Glasgow and from Inverness.

ACCOMMODATION

There are numerous hotels, B&Bs and self-catering options throughout Skye, and they come in various degrees of luxury, with, as you might expect, the greatest choice being in Portree, Broadford, Armadale and Uig. The Sligachan Hotel is a popular base for hill-goers.

There are a number of camp and caravan sites and no fewer than 16 hostels (11 independent and 5 SYHA) dotted across the island.

PUBLIC TRANSPORT

Most parts of the island are served reasonably well by local buses. In addition, postbus services operate between Broadford and Elgol, Dunvegan and Glendale, and Dunvegan and Gillen (further details available from main Post Office in Portree, telephone 01478 612533).

ORDNANCE SURVEY LANDRANGER MAPS

Landranger sheets 23, 32 and 33. Also, for those heading into the mountains, Outdoor Leisure Map 8 (1:25,000) *The Cuillin and Torridon Hills* is very useful.

MAIN PLACES OF INTEREST

Am Mám (1) Walk 6 and Short Walk 8

An Tuireann Arts Centre (2) Portree

Armadale Castle (3) Celebrated gardens and castle ruins, Armadale, Sleat

Bearreraig Bay (4) Walk 9

Bla Bheinn (5) Walk 6

Black Cuillin (6) Walk 6

Boreraig (township ruins) (7) Walk 5

Broch-Fiskavaig (8) Walk 8

Broch Sleadale (9) Walk 8

Camasunary Bay (10) Walk 6 and Short Walk 8

Cill Chriosd Kirk (11) Walk 5

Clan Donald Centre (12) Sited at Armadale Castle, Sleat

Coire Lagan (13) Walk 7

Coire Mhic Eachainn (14) Walk 10

Croft Museum (15) Luib, Loch Ainort

Dùn Beag Broch (16) Best-preserved Iron Age antiquity on Skye, at Struan

Dun Sgathaich Castle (17) Short Walk 7

Duntulm Castle (18) Coastal ruin on rocky headland at northwest tip of Trotternish peninsula. Amid the crumbling walls stands a cairn in memory of the MacArthurs, hereditary pipers to the Lords of the Isles

Dunvegan Castle (19) Popular tourist attraction at the head of Loch Dunvegan. Historic seat of Clan MacLeod since 1200

Environmental Centre (20) Broadford

Dunvegan Castle, Skye

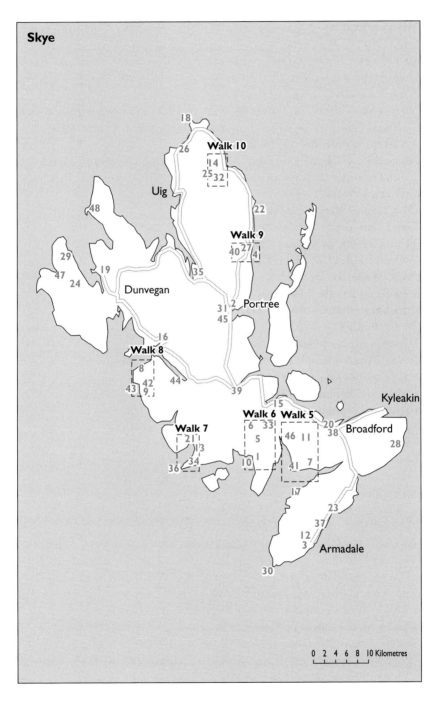

Skye

Glenbrittle (21) Spectacular mountain scenery of the Cuillin, at end of Glen Brittle road, at head of Loch Brittle (see also Walk 7)

Kilt Rock (22) Trotternish picnic spot on A855 with spectacular coastal views and waterfall

Knock Castle (23) Coastal ruin at Teangue, Sleat

MacLeod's Tables (24) North Table and South Table: distinctive flat-topped hills on Duirinish peninsula, both easily climbed from Osdale/Orbost.

Meall na Suiramach (25) Walk 10

Museum of Island Life and Monument to Flora MacDonald (26) Four restored blackhouses and burial place of Skye's heroine at Kilmuir, Trotternish

Old Man of Storr (27) Walk 9

Otter Sanctuary (28) Kylerhea, Sleat

Piping Heritage Centre (29) Borreraig, Dunvegan Head

Point of Sleat (30) Short Walk 6

Portree (31) Pretty environs of Skye's capital, especially the harbour (see Main Settlements, page 66)

Quiraing (32) Walk 10 and Short Walk 10

Red Cuillin (33) Walk 6

Rhundunan (34) Walk 7

River Snizort and Columba's Isle (35) A river island with ruins of St Columba's chapel. Short Walk 11

Rubh' an Dùnain (36) Walk 7

Rubh' an Dùnain, chambered cairn (36a) Walk 7

Sabhal Mor Ostaig (37) Gaelic college at Kilbeg, Sleat

Serpentarium (**Reptile Centre**) (38) Broadford

Sligachan (39) Focal point for walkers, with hotel and 'classic' mountain view of the Cuillin from picturesque old bridge

Storr, The (40) Walk 9

Suisnish (**township ruins**) (41) Walk 5

Talisker (**old village**) (42) Walk 8

Talisker Bay (43) Walk 8 and Short Walk 9

Talisker Distillery (44) Tours and whisky tasting at only distillery on Skye, Carbost, Minginish

The Aros Centre (45) Tourist centre in Portree that describes and explains stories, characters, events, etc, from the history of Skye. Includes forest walks

Torrin Marble Quarry (46) Walk 5

Toy Museum (47) Glendale, Duirinish

Trumpan Church (48) Ruins of a famous church on Waternish peninsula, burned by rampaging MacDonalds in 1578

Boreraig

Main interest and sights	Deserted townships, historical sites, coastal views and freshwater bird life: Cill Chriosd Kirk (11) Torrin Marble Quarry (46) Boreraig (7) Suisnish (41)
Route	Circular
Grade	Moderate
Map	OS Landranger sheet 32
Starting point	Cill Chriosd Kirk, GR 617208
Finishing point	As above
Distance	15.3 km/9$^1/_2$ mi (4$^1/_2$ hours)
Paths and terrain	A mix of rough and often wet paths and tracks of varying condition but ending on tarmac. Low-level walk with one or two moderate ascents. Walking boots recommended
Options	(a) from Cill Chriosd walk along the road in reverse of the main walk to Camas Malag. Go south on the track towards Suisnish but after 1.2 km/$^3/_4$ mi, follow the Allt nan Leac east to explore the caves of the limestone glen. At the top of the glen, join a vague path back to Cill Chriosd (moderate, 3$^1/_2$ hours) (b) drive down to Camas Malag and pursue the track to Suisnish. From the ruined township explore also coastal rocks at the shoreline at Suisnish Headland (Rubha Suisnish), returning same way (easy/moderate, 3 hours)
Nearby walks	Walk 6, Short Walk 8
Refreshments	None en route; nearest at Broadford

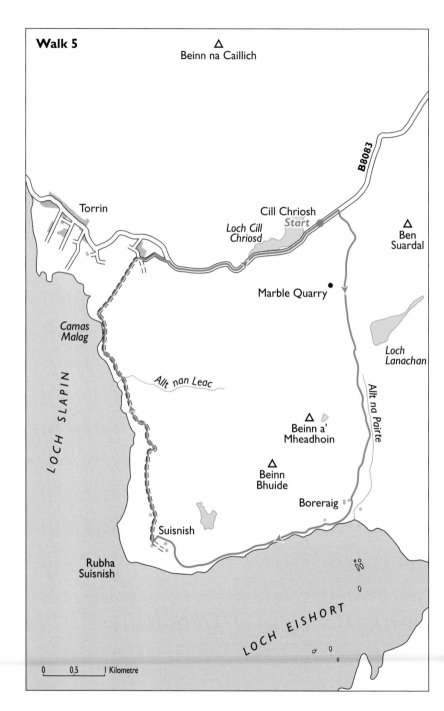

Walk 5

Beinn na Caillich

B8083

Torrin

Cill Chriosh
Start

*Loch Cill
Chriosd*

Ben
Suardal

Marble Quarry

*Camas
Malag*

Allt nan Leac

Loch
Lanachan

LOCH SLAPIN

Allt na Pairte

Beinn a'
Mheadhoin

Beinn
Bhuide

Boreraig

Suisnish

Rubha
Suisnish

LOCH EISHORT

0   0.5   I Kilometre

An Sgurr, Eigg

Kinloch Castle, Rum

The view of Eigg from the summit of Askival, Rum

The view of Rum from Laig, Eigg

The Cuillin from Elgol, Skye

The Red Cuillin from Bla Bheinn, Skye

Bla Bheinn and Loch Slapin, Skye

The Cuillin from Loch Brittle, Skye

The Pinnacles of The Storr, Trotternish, Skye

Museum of Island Life at Kilmuir, Skye

Grave slab at St Columba's Isle, Skye

River Talisker overlooked by Preshal More, Talisker, Skye

The Cuillin and the Sound of Raasay from Dùn Caan, Raasay

One of the stone mermaids at the battery by Raasay House, Raasay

When travelling on four wheels along the Broadford to Elgol road, you could be forgiven for surmising that the landmass which lies between Loch Eishort and Loch Slappin lacks obvious attractions. Exploration on two feet, however, reveals much of off-road interest, especially for lingerers among ruins and for those wishing to reflect on industrial heritage. For many, the highlights of this walk are found at the deserted ruins of the pre-clearance township of Boreraig, but west of here, the shores of two lochs provide the added bonus of some blissful coastal scenery.

Begin at the ivy-covered church ruins of **Cill Chriosd** (11). Together with its graveyard, this atmospheric site is worth a quick look before beginning the walk. Cill Chriosd was originally founded by St Maol Ruidh in the seventh century, with a new parish church established in the Middle Ages. The remains visible today date from the sixteenth century while the much older burial ground has long been a favourite final resting place for members of the MacKinnon and MacInnes clans.

Walk northeast along the road towards Broadford for a short distance, then take the first track on the right after the cattle grid. This leads on to a grassy path rising towards Ben Suardal. On reaching the track bed of a dismantled narrow gauge railway, turn right and follow it uphill, passing the abandoned sites of old quarry buildings, cuttings and slag heaps. Until the early twentieth century, the **Torrin Marble Quarry** (46) was very important, the high quality of its stone recognised in places far beyond Hebridean shores: Skye marble has been used in the Vatican and in the Palace of Versailles. Scaled-down commercial quarrying operations at Torrin continue today, but, because of the surrounding limestone, this area is also one of the most fertile parts of Skye.

From where the railway track bed appears to terminate (20 minutes), continue along a path up to the left. The gradient levels out higher up, close to Loch Lonachan, but having ventured farther south, begin to gradually descend alongside the west bank of the Allt na Pairte. Go over a small rise and then drop down more sharply towards the sea at Loch Eishort.

Close to Loch Eishort lies the deserted but well-preserved crofting village of **Boreraig** (7) (1hour, 20 minutes), the remains of which are spread over a wide area just above the shore. It is humbling to remember the people who once inhabited these cottages and who would have endured a level of hardship that it is impossible for us to imagine today. Such reflection on the struggles of the past adds yet greater poignancy to the eerie atmosphere of Boreraig, heightening further one's sense of desolation in the landscape.

Bear right towards the west side of the village, making short leaps to cross a couple of burns. The promontory of Dùn Boreraig overlooks the sea, but the dun is now of little note as an antiquity. Without deviation continue west along the path that hugs the rocky shoreline. Views to the Sleat peninsula across Loch Eishort on your left and attractive waterfalls tumbling to the sea from the cliffs on your right are among the scenic pleasures to be enjoyed on the walk around to the next abandoned village, **Suisnish** (41).

Approaching Suisnish Point (Rubha Suisnish), the path rises up above coastal crags at the foot of Carn Dearg. Veer north and follow the perimeter of the enclosure uphill, turning sharp left at the top. Then go through the second gate on the left and drop down towards an abandoned red-roofed cottage ($2^{1}/_{4}$ hours). Here, join the track heading north from Suisnish. This track provides 3.5 km/$2^{1}/_{4}$ mi of easy walking above Loch Slapin, with superb views to the dramatic mountain of Bla Bheinn (Walk 6) as well as to the rounded hills of the Red Cuillin.

At the scenic bay of Camas Malag, turn inland, passing close to the still operational quarry workings at Torrin. Having rejoined the road at Kilbride, finish by walking along the tarmac road that passes between the woodland at Coille Gaireallach and the freshwater of Loch Cill Chriosd. In their own ways, both sites are fascinating for the flora and fauna to be found: the woodland for its deciduous mix of hazel, birch and rowan as well as lime-loving flowers, including orchids; and the loch also for its diversity of vegetation and for tiny dabchicks and wintering whooper swans.

Bla Bheinn

Main interest and sights	Fantastic mountainscapes and superb coastal views: Bla Bheinn (5) Am Mám Pass (1) Camasunary Bay (10) Black Cuillin (6) Red Cuillin (33)
Route	Linear
Grade	Strenuous
Map	OS Landranger sheet 32
Starting point	Kilmarie; parking bay on B8083, GR 545172
Finishing point	As above
Distance	13 km/8 mi (6¹/₄ hours)
Paths and terrain	Easily followed rough track to Am Mám followed by path to base of mountain. Relatively difficult and steep terrain on south ridge of Bla Bheinn. Walking boots essential
Options	(a) Main summit of Bla Bheinn (see main text, page 77 – extra 40 minutes) (b) Loch Coruisk – one of the finest coastal walks in Scotland. Low level all the way. From Am Mám descend to Camasunary Bay and continue around coast to Loch Coruisk via the Bad Step (a scramble). Return the same way (moderate/strenuous, 6 hours) (c) The coast from Camasunary – use the coastal path to Elgol, returning to Kilmarie along B8083. (moderate, 4³/₄ hours)
Nearby walks	Walk 5, Short Walk 8
Refreshments	None en route; nearest at Elgol or Broadford

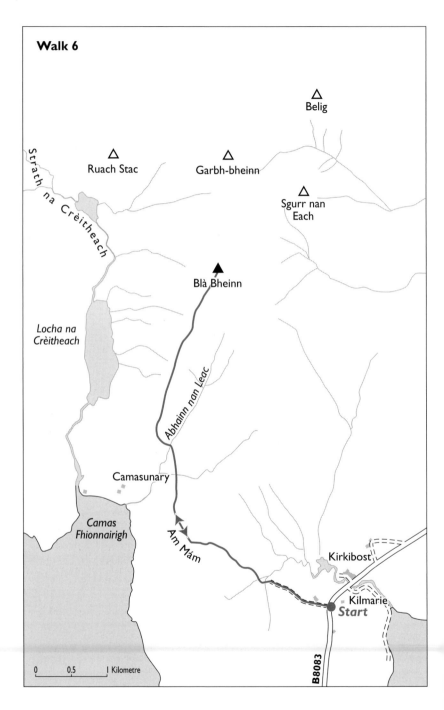

Walk 6

Belig

Ruach Stac

Garbh-bheinn

Sgurr nan Each

Strath na Crèitheach

Blà Bheinn

Locha na Crèitheach

Abhainn nan Leac

Camasunary

Camas Fhionnairigh

Am Mám

Kirkibost

Kilmarie
Start

B8083

0   0.5   I Kilometre

No fewer than thirteen peaks (eleven of them Munros – peaks over 3,000 ft/914.4 m) make up the magnificent and much celebrated range of mountains known as the Black Cuillin. Walking routes up on to any of their summits, or along the ridges between them, are typically long and technically difficult. The Cuillin presents the most formidable of hillwalking challenges in the British Isles. Only one or two chinks in its 12 km/7^1/$_2$ mi chain of sheer buttresses, knife-edge ridges and sharp, seemingly insurmountable pinnacles exist, but even these are beyond the parameters of this guidebook. With the compass-deflecting properties of the iron-rich gabbro making navigation in bad weather unreliable, the challenges of the Cuillin are such as to render the territory out of bounds to all but the most committed and capable of mountaineers. So we need to look a little beyond the main range, to the Cuillin outliers, for a mountain within the grasp of non-scrambling, non-climbing hill-goers.

To the east of the main ridge, there rises a separate mountain in its own right, which, on one side, offers a relatively straightforward route to and from its summit. The view of the Cuillin from there is incomparable and, by popular consent in mountaineering circles, is heralded as 'the finest mountain on Skye'. The mountain is **Bla Bheinn** (5) the south ridge of which is considered an 'easy' route by Skye standards. Nonetheless, its ascent is the most difficult and strenuous walk in this guide so only attempt it if you have experience of Munros.

From the parking bay, walk across the road and gain the track leading west-northwest. In the dip on your right, near Kirkibost, beside a lochan, still standing upright are three stones of the circle of Na Clachan Bhreige. Being almost completely surrounded by water, however, the site is not easy to approach.

The track gently ascends to the pass of **Am Mám** (1). From the top of the pass, at 189 m/620 ft, the sharp and jagged skyline across **Camasunary Bay** (10) comes into view. Climb a little way up on to the bank on the right to see it more clearly. The juxtaposition of coast and mountain at Loch Scavaig presents a scene of spectacular drama, a wilderness possibly unmatched in the British Isles for its rugged grandeur. But to appreciate the **Black Cuillin** (6) to its fullest extent, it is better to attempt to climb even higher still.

From the Am Mám, the track descends to the bay, but proceed only as far as the hairpin bend and from there continue north on the path to the Abhainn nan Leac. Soon after crossing this river, strike off to the right, climbing directly up the south ridge of Bla Bheinn. Although the path is not always obvious, the ridge is well defined. Any rocky knolls obstructing your ascent are best passed by skirting around the east side of them. This will involve some careful footwork and some clambering about on rocks, so be very attentive. Be careful also of the sheer gullies and ravines on the west side.

The true extent of the unbroken outline of the Black Cuillin is revealed once you have gained about 500 m/1,640 ft of height, where, for fun, you might wish to try to identify all the peaks of the range, from Gars-bheinn at the south end to Sgurr nan Gillean at the northern tip. The end-to-end ridge traverse of the range is considered to be the finest mountain expedition possible in Britain, and your viewpoint will help you to appreciate why. But do be sure to keep one eye on the mountain you are standing on as the gullies and ravines continue to drop away sharply on the west side.

The magnificent panorama from the southwest summit (3^1/$_4$ hours) reveals some striking contrasts in the mountains that demarcate Glen Sligachan. This is because of differing igneous geologies, the Black Cuillin gabbros being dark, very hard and, as mentioned above, eroded into sharp pinnacles and ridges, whereas the Red Hills, or **Red Cuillin** (33), on the east side of the glen, are of granite and have worn to form less distinct, gently rounded hills. But the view extends even farther to the north, across to the Inner Sound and the island of Raasay (see Walks 11 to 13) and to the south, most notably to Rum and the Small Isles.

The main summit of Bla Bheinn is just 300 m farther north, tantalisingly close but for ordinary mortals perhaps a summit too far. To reach it, however, first descend an awkward and potentially treacherous drop through a rocky gully leading down to the col between the two summits. From there it is easy to ascend a final section of ridge leading up to the trig pillar. Having gained just a further 2 m/6 ft over the south summit, the view is little improved upon. Nonetheless, committed Munroists should allow an extra 30 minutes at least. Return from Bla Bheinn by walking back down the south ridge.

Headland of Rubh' an Dùnain

Main interest and sights	Iron Age antiquities and very fine views of the Cuillin and to the Small Isles: Coire Lagan (13) Rubh' an Dùnain (36) Rubh' an Dùnain Chambered Cairn (36a) Rhundunan (optional) (34)
Route	Linear/circular
Grade	Easy/moderate
Map	OS Landranger sheet 32
Starting point	End of Glen Brittle road at Loch Brittle, GR 409207
Finishing point	As above
Distance	13 km/8 mi (4^1/$_2$ hours)
Paths and terrain	Clearly marked path to and from the Slochd Dubh. Unpathed and in places wet around tip of the headland but nowhere difficult; without significant gradient. Walking boots recommended
Options	(a) Return from Rubh' an Dùnain via farm remains of **Rhundunan** (34) encountered 400 m/^{1}/$_4$ mi northeast of the cave. Path from there goes north to Loch Brittle (b) **Coire Lagan** (13) – A path goes east from campsite, rising steeply to the lochan in the corrie at 570 m/1,870 ft, a fantastic setting. Proceeding beyond is for mountaineers only. Return same way (moderate/strenuous, 4 hours)
Nearby walks	None
Refreshments	None en route; nearest at Carbost

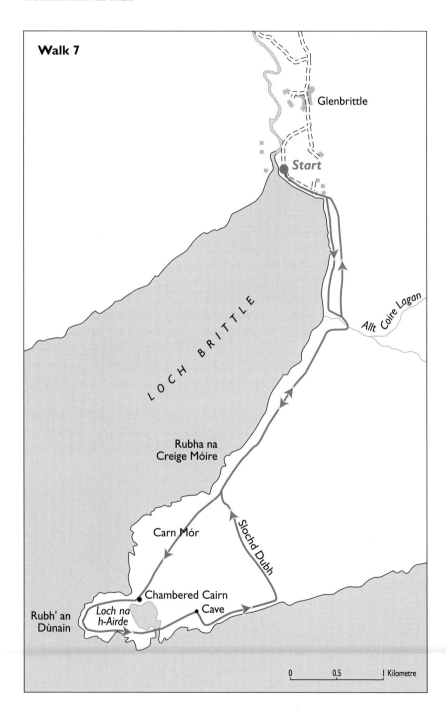

Walk 7

Glenbrittle

Start

Allt Coire Lagan

L O C H   B R I T T L E

Rubha na
Creige Móire

Carn Mór

Slochd Dubh

Chambered Cairn

Cave

Rubh' an
Dùnain

Loch na
h-Airde

0   0.5   1 Kilometre

At the remote headland of **Rubh' an Dùnain** (36) one experiences a feeling of isolation hard to come by elsewhere on the island. This also happens to be the chunk of Skye closest to the island of Rum, but on this walk one's gaze is drawn in other directions as well. Rubh' an Dùnain lies in the shadow of the magnificent Black Cuillin. This is the kind of place where poets are inspired, where the shifting play of Hebridean light on mountain and sea can be mesmerising. With the added intrigue of a Neolithic antiquity, there is much to enjoy on Rubh' an Dùnain.

Set off on the Glen Brittle campsite track, at first heading directly towards the mighty Cuillin. From the east end of the beach at the head of Loch Brittle, gain the lower of the two paths that head south beside the shore of the loch. Stay close to the shoreline until reaching the Allt Coire Lagan, then cross this stream at a footbridge higher up. Climb a little higher still to get on to the better path. Turn right and continue along the coast but not before first taking in the breathtaking drama of the **Coire Lagan** (13), dominating the scene, surrounded by a ring of truly awesome peaks. Among them is Sgurr Alasdair, at 992 m/3,256 ft the highest peak of the Cuillin. Not surprisingly, the Coire Lagan is one of the most visited corries of the range although the mountain tops are pretty much out of bounds to average walkers.

The path gradually rises above cliffs at Rubha na Creige Móire (1 hour), at the same time skirting below the low escarpment of Creag Mhór. Where the path forks, keep to the lower one. On reaching the Slochd Dubh ('Black Ditch'), a long, narrow trench-like feature cutting right across the headland, the path veers left. Here, strike off right through the gap breaching the drystone wall, continuing over the wet grass and around to the left side of Carn Mór. Drop down through an obvious gap on the other side and then walk south towards Loch na h-Airde.

At the loch, you will notice a small wall leading out to the bay of Camas a Mhúrain while just in front of it rises the Neolithic mound of **Rubh' an Dùnain Chambered Cairn** (36a) (1³/₄ hours). Dating from the third and early second millennia BC, this cairn is a very fine and well-preserved example of a passage grave. The central chamber can be entered on the southeast side or down through the open top. Investigation of the intact walls of the chamber reveals a dark, damp but sheltered microclimate where ferns and liverworts are flourishing in gaps between the lintels. A second but less significant unchambered cairn can be found just a few metres to the west.

To reach the very best vantage point, venture a little farther west, beyond Loch na h-Airde, up out on to the tip of the headland (2 hours). In fine weather it is a place that encourages lingerers. I once spent a memorable hour on Rubh' an Dùnain, enraptured by fluctuating shafts of sunlight over the mountains of Rum, some 12 km/7 mi distant. Here, in reasonably warm December sunshine, I picnicked on the turf. In the other direction the mountain range of the Cuillin had turned dark and brooding under its own blanket of clouds and powdered by the first snows of winter. Such moments may stir the hearts of poets, when even the most pragmatic are at least reminded of the eccentricities of Hebridean weather.

For the visually aware, the Cuillin mountains make a fitting subject for the camera, especially if you can frame something of Loch Brittle in the foreground.

Make your way around to the south side of Loch na h-Airde. To reach the cave seen up in the rocks above bracken, walk 350 m due east-northeast from the crossing of the channel of water that connects the loch to the sea. This site is noteworthy for Beaker pottery found here in 1932.

From the cave a choice of two routes is possible for heading back north to the shore of Loch Brittle, with negligible difference in either time or distance. Those who appreciate ruins, can return via what was once the farm of Rhundunan (see Options). Otherwise, go east across the undulating terrain that rises above the sea cliffs as far as the south end of the Slochd Dubh (3 hours) and the stream named after it, the Allt an t-Sluichd Dhuibh. Birdwatchers should have their binoculars handy as there is always the chance of spotting a very rare sea eagle, most likely to be seen circling high in the sky above Soay Sound. At the Slochd Dubh, simply follow the path alongside the drystone dyke running northwest through the 'trench' to return to the Loch Brittle path. For a slight variation on your way back to Glen Brittle, keep on the better, higher path between the Allt Coire Lagan and the campsite.

Talisker Bay

Main interest and sights	Interesting flora and fauna, unusual topography and a long history of human habitation: Talisker Bay (43) Talisker (old village) (42) Broch (Fiskavaig – optional) (8) Broch (Sleadale – optional) (9)
Route	Linear
Grade	Easy/moderate
Map	OS Landranger sheet 32
Starting point	Fiskavaig, at hairpin bend near end of road, GR 323332
Finishing point	Fiskavaig
Distance	9 km/5$^1/_2$ mi (3$^1/_2$ hours)
Paths and terrain	Mostly good level surfaces although wet at Huisgill. Steep but short descent and re-ascent to and from River Talisker
Options	(a) **Broch at Fiskavaig** (8) – From near start of path, walk northwest across pathless moor towards a prominent basalt tor. Great view across Loch Bracadale and beyond (extra 30 minutes there and back) (b) **Broch at Sleadale** (9) – Walk south above west side of Sleadale Burn, veering right after about 600 m/$^3/_8$ mi to the ruins (extra hour there and back)
Nearby walks	Short Walk 9 may be combined with this walk
Refreshments	Bay View Guest House, Talisker (great nettle beer!); otherwise, Portnalong or Carbost

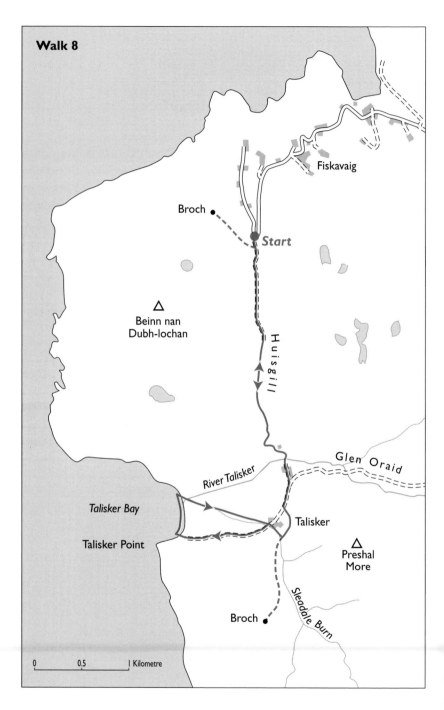

Walk 8

Fiskavaig

Broch •

● **Start**

△
Beinn nan
Dubh-lochan

H u i s g i l l

G l e n   O r a i d

River Talisker

Talisker Bay

Talisker

Talisker Point

△
Preshal
More

Broch •

Sleadale Burn

0   0.5   I Kilometre

The Minginish peninsula is often overlooked by visitors to Skye. Those few who do venture west from Glen Brittle, or detour from the A863 in Glen Drynoch, are invariably attracted by the lure of the whisky distillery at Carbost and little else beyond.

Tranquil and secluded, **Talisker Bay** (43) is hidden away at the bottom of Gleann Oraid. Here, where the River Talisker meets the sea, a lush, flat plain has been formed, although according to local legend not by the erosive force of the river. It is said that the Irish giant Fyn McColl, when he stepped across to Skye from the Giants' Causeway in Ireland, having first visited Staffa, left his footprint here. Today, Talisker is a peaceful haven, where coastal rejuvenation and pastoral calm come in equal measure. Talisker Bay harbours a few surprises in its landscape as well as more than a few delicate treasures in its natural history.

Leave the tarmac at the hairpin bend and follow a farm track south. Head towards Preshal Mor, a prominent stack of basalt some 3 km/2 mi distant. After crossing a burn, the ground becomes wetter underfoot but the walking remains easy. Descend a series of zigzags to Gleann Oraid, the valley of the River Talisker. This green and lush flood plain suggests a fertile place. Indeed, barley was once grown here for the Talisker distillery.

The towering upthrust of lava that has formed Preshal Mor dominates Talisker. Among the buildings on the south side of the river is the Bay View Guest House ($^3/_4$ hour). It is on the left side of the track and I can highly recommend a break here for sandwiches and nettle beer although perhaps you should earn it by first exploring more of Talisker and the bay.

From the end of the road in Gleann Oraid, first make a brief detour from the track that leads to the beach. Look out for a gate on the left, opposite the horse chestnut and sycamore trees. This provides access to the hill slope below Preshal Mor. Walk up towards an obvious square enclosure, the grave of 'James Thomas Cameron of Talisker', the owner of Talisker House who died in 1946. Proceeding a further 200 m east-southeast will bring you to the fallen ruins of the old village of **Talisker** (42) ($1^1/_4$ hours). In the early nineteenth century, there were over 200 people living in the glen compared to no more than twenty today.

Descend towards the Sleadale Burn and follow it downstream to regain the track by Talisker House. Continue west from here to reach the beach. Like other beaches on Skye, the sands of Talisker Bay ($1^3/_4$ hours) are grey and rather drab. Nevertheless, removing shoes and socks and paddling at the water's edge is a tempting distraction on a warm day. Boot-loose and fancy free, make your way across the bay in a northerly direction towards an impressive waterfall that cascades from cliff top to sea. The coastal scenery is delightful, and beachcombing for zeolites, silica-based crystals associated with lava flows, is a common pastime here. Fortunately, Talisker is now a more peaceful place than it was in the early nineteenth century. The then owner of Talisker House, Colonel Cameron, had a full-time piper playing at Talisker Point. In recognition of the musician's efforts, the well near the gate at the beach is known as 'Piper's Well'.

From the mouth of the River Talisker, walk up along the path that follows the Sleadale Burn, the stream on the right. In springtime, the water meadows are splashed with a lovely profusion of colours provided by irises, kingcups, bluebells, wood anemones, primroses and orchids. And in summertime there is a chance of seeing a real rarity on the wing, the Talisker Burnet moth (*Zygaena lonicerae*), a subspecies found nowhere else and all the more unusual among moths for being active in daylight. Otters are also frequently seen in the vicinity while eyes turned to the sky might spot a golden eagle. Eagles are known to have regularly nested in the glen and very occasionally sea eagles are seen at Talisker.

The path terminates by the trees at Talisker House ($2^1/2$ hours). Here, turn left on rejoining the track back to the bridge over the river. A short, sharp climb leads up to Huisgill again, and from here the return to Fiskavaig continues in reverse of the outward ramble.

Loch Bracadale, Skye

W A L K 9

The Old Man of Storr and Bearreraig Bay

Main interest and sights	A fabulous assemblage of rock pinnacles in an elevated escarpment and an opportunity for fossil hunting at sea level: The Storr (40) Old Man of Storr (27) Bearreraig Bay (4)
Route	Circular
Grade	Moderate
Map	OS Landranger sheet 23
Starting point	Car park immediately north of Loch Leathan, GR 508525
Finishing point	As above
Distance	9 km/5³/₄ mi (4 hours)
Paths and terrain	All paths are steep, particularly those to and from the Coire Faoin and the path to Bearreraig Bay. Wet ground in the forest but no other difficulties
Options	(a) By returning to the parking place before visiting Bearreraig Bay, this walk divides itself nicely into two short walks. Old Man of Storr only (moderate, 2¹/₂ hours); Bearreraig Bay only (easy, 1¹/₂ hours) (b) From the Old Man, climb north and above the cliffs then turn back and follow cliff edge up to reach summit of The Storr. Return on south side, descending to road and Bearreraig Bay from Bealach Beag (moderate/strenuous; 5 hours)
Nearby walks	None; nearest are Walk 10 and Short Walk 10
Refreshments	None en route; nearest at hotels, bars, cafés and shops in Portree.

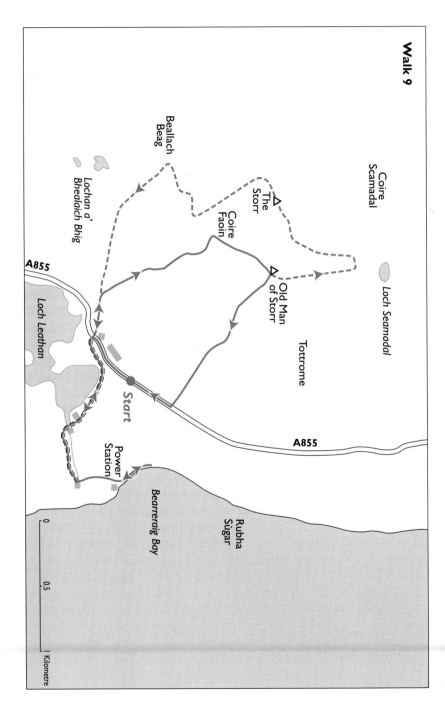

Trotternish is the northernmost district of Skye. An almost continuous line of basalt cliffs forms the long, steep escarpment of the Trotternish Ridge, essentially the backbone of the peninsula. It is a dramatic landscape when seen from the main road below, but its most spectacular features demand to be seen at close quarters. While the two-day trek along the crest of the ridge is considered one of the finest high-level expeditions in Scotland, there exist numerous less challenging shorter walks amidst the intriguing landslips and isolated pinnacles of Trotternish. **The Storr** (40) is the highest summit on the 38 km/24 mile-long ridge, but it is the remarkable pillar of rock below it, the **Old Man of Storr** (27), that attracts far more curiosity. This walk visits that topographical wonderland as well as including the geological interest at **Bearreraig Bay** (4).

From the car park, walk southwest along the road to reach a kissing gate on the right, just beyond a house. Above the gate, ascend a clearly defined path up along the edge of a plantation. To avoid any waterlogged ground, weave a way between the spruce trees on the right. At the uppermost reaches of the forested area, gain a path that continues rising more steeply to Coire Faoin. Bear right as you approach this rock sanctuary, venturing at will along any of a tangle of paths among the weirdest basalt formations. It is a truly wonderful

The Old Man of Storr, Skye

landscape in which the Old Man is the most conspicuous feature, a precariously poised 50 m/165 ft-high splinter of rock ($1^1/4$ hours).

The atmosphere of the Coire Faoin affects all those who linger. To stand here below the dark curtain of cliffs and assemblage of crumbling volcanic spires, is to feel that you have come upon a unique natural theatre, a stage set carved in basalt. The performance is silent yet evocative, occasionally interrupted by the echoing repertoire of ring ouzels calling to one another. The Old Man himself seems almost to defy gravity, teetering on an undercut plinth of bedrock while a neighbouring monolith comes complete with sharp fangs and a rock window.

Option (b) is highly recommended, but if you've seen enough, leave the sanctuary and descend to the road by a path along the northern edge of the plantation. Turn right to reach the car park, which is about 800 m/$^1/2$ mi back along the road ($2^1/2$ hours). Alternatively, return by the ascent route.

To get to Bearreraig Bay, walk on past the car park and pursue the track off to the left that leads, via the north shore of Loch Leathan, to a dam. Go over the dam and follow a track east. From the hydroelectric building at the end, a sign points the way to 'Footpath and Viewpoint'. The viewpoint (3 hours) is just another 100 m beyond and from it there is an excellent view across the Sound of Raasay to the Torridon mountains on the distant mainland.

Information panels explain the fascinating geology of Bearreraig Bay, its dramatic 160 m/500 ft-high cliffs rising sheer from the sea below you. The igneous rocks exhibit a distinct banding above older Jurassic sediments, but it is down on the beach that one has the opportunity for more personal discoveries. Among the rocks and pebbles there are fossils of prehistoric sea creatures to be found, including ammonites and belemnites. A new steep path descends to the beach ($3^1/4$ hours – the 640 steps leading down to the power station at sea level are no longer considered safe), but remember you will have to climb back up. From the viewpoint return the same way.

WALK 10

The Landslips of the Quiraing

Main interest and sights	A Tolkeinesque landscape of slipped and detached rock: Quiraing (32) Coire Mhic Eachainn (14) Meall na Suiramach (25)
Route	Circular
Grade	Moderate/strenuous
Map	OS Landranger sheet 23
Starting point	Parking bay off of A855, 1 km/²/₃ mi south of Flodigarry, GR 463711
Finishing point	As above
Distance	10 km/6¹/₄ mi (4¹/₄ hours)
Paths and terrain	Clear well-worn path in vicinity of Quiraing and below Meall na Suiramach; more difficult terrain near Loch Hasco. Steep climbs on to the various pinnacles and up to Meall na Suiramach
Options	The options below are both up-and-down-again additions to the main walk: (a) The Prison – climb up south wall and follow path across to the base of its highest pinnacle followed by scramble: a situation not for the faint-hearted (extra 25 minutes) (b) The Table and The Needle – gain the base of The Needle by climbing the steep slope from the main path. Beyond it, go through breach in rock wall to find way up on to The Table (extra 1 hour)
Nearby walks	Short Walk 10 (easy walk to the Quiraing)
Refreshments	None en route; nearest at hotel at Flodigarry

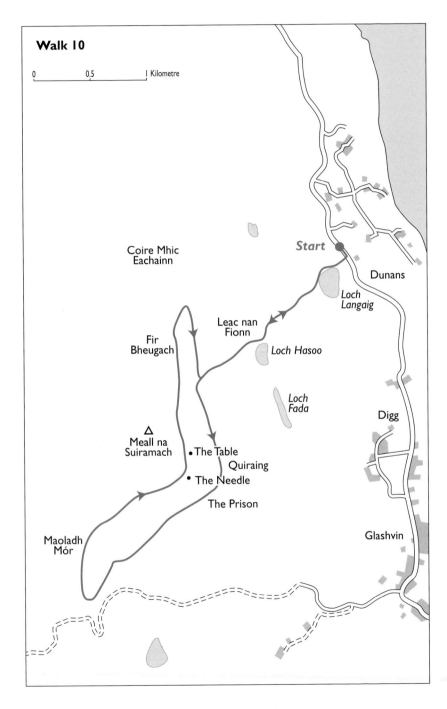

Walk 10

0   0.5   1 Kilometre

Coire Mhic
Eachainn

Start

Dunans

*Loch
Langaig*

Leac nan
Fionn

Fir
Bheugach

Loch Hasoo

*Loch
Fada*

Digg

Δ
Meall na
Suiramach

• The Table

Quiraing

• The Needle

The Prison

Maoladh
Mór

Glashvin

The lava still flows at the north end of Skye, albeit that it no longer spills from volcanoes and its movements are perceptible only in geological time. Nevertheless, the east-facing escarpment rock of the Trotternish Ridge represents the largest ongoing land slippage in Britain. The **Quiraing** (32), at the northern extremity of that ridge, is the most spectacular expression of this landslide. The proximity of the Quiraing to the Brogaig to Uig road means that the area is easily accessible from the south and consequently it is one of Skye's most popular walks (Short Walk 10). However, a more interesting and less frequented approach is possible from the north.

At first walk south from the parking bay but leave the road after about 100 m for a path that leads towards the escarpment. This passes the north shore of Loch Langaig and then ascends to the enclosed hollow of Loch Hasco. From the shore of the latter, follow a steeply rising fence line on the south flank of Leac nan Fionn. From the top continue across country and along faint paths aiming for the Trotternish escarpment.

A more obvious path, running north to south, is encountered when directly below the escarpment ($^3/_4$ hour). Here, turn left and within another 15 minutes the fabulous features of the most spectacular section of the Quiraing are reached. High up on a steep slope to your right is the sharp pinnacle of The Needle and, hidden behind it, The Table, while on your immediate left is The Prison. All justify closer inspection, especially the experience of being on The Table, but you will need to set aside extra time and energy for this (see Options).

A very steep slope leads up to the base of The Needle, and The Table lies beyond it. However, The Table and many other features of the Quiraing are best seen from above, from **Meall na Suiramach** (25). The Prison is closer to hand and an extremely rewarding distraction for scramblers and those with a good head for heights.

From the base of The Prison walk southwest along the 'tourist route' towards the road and the car park at the top of the pass. Just before the car park, pursue a path that rises steeply on the right and continue climbing northwards, close to the cliff edge. There is a cairn at the top of the escarpment, and looking down one appreciates the remarkable flatness of The Table. Here, on this elevated grassy plateau, cattle were once hidden from pillaging Norsemen. In more peaceful times, The Table has been used as a shinty pitch. Its enclosed setting could hardly be more dramatic, encircled as it is by vertical walls of rock and sharp basaltic fins. Such a magnificent assemblage of broken and detached escarpment rocks, a slipped landscape sculpted over millions of years by volcano, glacier and ocean, is unique in Britain.

Continue the walk heading north, descending to the **Coire Mhic Eachainn**

(14) while enjoying the wonderful views out over the Minch to the Outer Hebrides. After a little more than 1 km/^{2}/$_3$ mi of descent, take the path on the right turning back sharply south. This leads below the escarpment again. After going through a gap in a drystone wall, you will soon have returned to the route out (in reverse of the approach via Lochs Hasco and Langaig).

Short Walks

6 POINT OF SLEAT (2¹⁄₄ HOURS; OSLR MAP 32)

The **Point of Sleat** (30) is the headland at the wind-lashed extremity that juts into the sea at the tip of the Garden of Skye. A 3 km/2 mi-long moorland track leads west from the end of the road at the Aird of Sleat to the tiny fishing inlet at Acairseid an Rubha. Eigg and Rum are seen clearly from here, specially if you climb an extra 30 m/100 ft to the top of the rise immediately to the south of the inlet. Return by the same track.

If you can muster a little more energy on this outing, continue all the way to the lighthouse at the Point of Sleat. This brings even greater rewards in terms of fabulous coastline and seaward views (allow an extra hour).

7 DÙN SGATHAICH (I HOUR; OSLR MAP 32)

Dùn Sgathaich (17) is probably the earliest of Skye's castles. Said to have been built in a single night either by fairies, by a witch or by the Irish warrior Cuchullin, depending on which legend you favour, the castle is also said to have once been protected by a pit full of snakes and beaked toads. It may have, in fact, had Norse origins, but beyond doubt is the fact that the castle occupies a commanding position on a coastal stack overlooking Loch Eishort.

A track and a path go west from the road at Tokavaig (GR 601118) to the headland. Part of the walls of the castle stand 5 m/16 ft high and can be viewed from the landward side of the stack on which it stands. However, with careful manoeuvring, it is still possible to cross the narrow ledge left by the collapsed arches of a connecting wall. The island of Rum lies out in the Sea of the Hebrides, but the principal purpose of Dun Sgathaich must have been defensive, as a lookout across the Skye coast and to the entrances of two potentially significant sea lochs, Loch Slapin and Loch Eishort.

8 CAMASUNARY BAY (2¹⁄₂ HOURS; OSLR MAP 32)

Follow the track from Kilmarie as for Walk 6 to the pass of **Am Mám** (1). From the hairpin bend just beyond the top of the pass, continue down the track to enjoy the seclusion of **Camasunary Bay** (10). For most, it will be the sight of the mountains from Am Mám that provides the highlight of this short walk, but the extensive shingle beach and flat grass behind it offer a pleasurable respite from all the hills. Unfortunately, a shameful disregard for Scotland's marine environment is all too evident: plastic bottles, nylon netting and acres of polythene litter the beach at Camasunary.

9 ABOVE TALISKER BAY (2 HOURS; OSLR MAP 32)

Park at Talisker at the end of the road in Gleann Oraid (GR 327306). Walk
north to cross the River Talisker at the bridge, then ascend the flank of the
hill of Sròn Mhór. At the top walk west, passing above the waterfall to reach
the headland at Rubha Cruinn. The view across **Talisker Bay** (43) and to the
coastal cliffs beyond is, on a clear still summer evening, quite divine. This
shortie is easily combined with Walk 8.

10 THE QUIRAING (1 1/4 HOURS; OSLR MAP 23)

This short walk visits the fabulous landslip features of Trotternish described
in Walk 10. It utilises the quick, easy and more popular approach from the
upper car park on the road between Brogaig and Uig. Simply follow the path
northeast, below the escarpment, in reverse of the southernmost section of
the main walk. To make a circuit, return from The Prison by the more east-
erly path to gain the road at the lower car park.

11 RIVER SNIZORT AND ST COLUMBA'S ISLE (1 HOUR; OSLR MAP 23)

St Columba's Isle (35) sits in the **River Snizort** (35), near its estuary at
Skeabost. Located at GR 418485, it is simply marked as 'chapel' on the map,
yet it is probably the most historically significant site on Skye. The crumbling
remains of a chapel, as well as of the fallen walls of other parts of this ancient
ecclesiastical complex, are still to be seen, as are one or two exceptionally
well-preserved grave slabs.

St Columba's Isle was the site of the cathedral church of the Bishops of the
Isles for more than 400 years. Established upon the consecration of Wymond
(Hamond), Bishop of Skye, in 1079, the Bishopric remained here until 1498,
when it was moved to Iona. One particularly harrowing tale recounts a medieval family quarrel, an episode of capture and mutilation among Norse
relatives. In 1223, Godred Donn, son of the Norse King of the Isles and Man,
was captured by his uncle, Olav the Black, on St Columba's Isle. Godred survived in spite of being tortured, including having his eyes put out.

Park near to the east of the entrance of Skeabost House (hotel), just off the
A850 (GR 419484). Walk over the old road bridge that spans the River
Snizort, then go down a path on the left that leads to the footbridge giving
access to St Columba's Isle. To continue the walk, make your way along the
north bank of the river, weaving a way between birch trees as far as where the
river empties into Loch Snizort Beag. The remains of an old settlement are
still discernible in the undergrowth, including a rusty iron cogwheel in what
was once presumably a working mill. A tarmac road, a little to the north, allows for a speedy return.

Raasay

For those prepared to spend at least two or three days on the island, Raasay is richly rewarding. Lying just 3 km/2 mi east of Skye, it benefits from the protection offered by the larger island. The winds are lighter and the skies clearer, a weather shadow that aids the proliferation of a luxuriant and rare flora. Favourable conditions for plants were further enhanced by the fact that much of the island managed to escape glaciation and therefore retained the vital nutrients in its top soil.

Whilst the interior is hilly, the coastal fringes of the south are relatively fertile, characteristic of a sandstone and limestone geology. An attractive mix of trees cling to slopes above Churchton Bay, a forest fringed by fuchsia and rhododendron. Old chapel remains, an ancient broch, underground chambers and garden statues are all to be found among the encroaching undergrowth in the vicinity of Raasay House (Short Walk 12). The north end of the island is more barren and exposed. Here is a land carved from hard, grey gneiss rock with relatively few areas of leafy vegetation other than where rowan, birch scrub and bracken have managed to secure a foothold.

The definitive feature of Raasay is its flat-topped hill, Dùn Caan (Walk 12). There can be few better places for admiring the mountains of Skye than its summit.

MAIN SETTLEMENTS
Almost the entire population of 160 live within 2.5 km/1¹/₂ mi of the main village, Inverarish. Here there is a post office, a general store, a primary school and the only hotel. The best sources of information are at **Raasay Heritage Museum** (11) (Jen Barnet and Rob Mackay, telephone 01478 660207) or from Margaret Moodie (35 Inverarish Terrace, telephone 01478 660295).

ACCESS
A Cal Mac vehicle and passenger ferry, the *Loch Striven*, serves East Suisnish on Raasay. The crossing from Sconser on Skye takes 15 minutes, with the ferry operating several times daily except Sunday.

ACCOMMODATION
B&B is available at the Isle of Raasay Hotel (telephone 01478 660222) or at Churchton House (telephone 01478 660260). There is a cosy – if basic –

SYHA hostel, the Allan Evans' Memorial Hostel (telephone 01478 660240), 2 km/1¼ mi north and up the hill from Inverarish, near Oskaig. It has 30 bunks.

PUBLIC TRANSPORT
From Inverarish a single strip of tarmac runs north along the length of the island as far as Arnish. There is no public transport of any kind, so taking a private vehicle is worth considering, especially if you wish to explore the north end.

ORDNANCE SURVEY LANDRANGER MAPS
Landranger sheet 24 covers all of Raasay.

MAIN PLACES OF INTEREST
Battery, The (1) Short Walk 12
Beinn na h-Iolaire (2) Walk 13
Beinn na' Leac (3) Walk 11
Druim an Aonaich (4) Walk 11
Dùn Borodale (5) Short Walk 12
Dùn Caan (6) Walk 12
Eilean Fladday (7) Walk 13
Forest Walk (8) Waymarked walk in Raasay Forest
Fountain Pond (9) Short Walk 12
Hallaig (10) Walk 11
Heritage Museum (11) Short Walk 12
Loch na Mna (12) Walk 12
North Fearns (13) Walk 11
Pictish Stone (14) Short Walk 12
Raasay House (15) Short Walk 12
Raasay Iron Mine (16) Walk 12
Stable buildings (17) Short Walk 12
St Moluag's Chapel (18) Short Walk 12
Temptation Hill (19) Short Walk 12
Torran Woods (20) Walk 13
Uamhna Ramh Souterrain (21) Short Walk 12

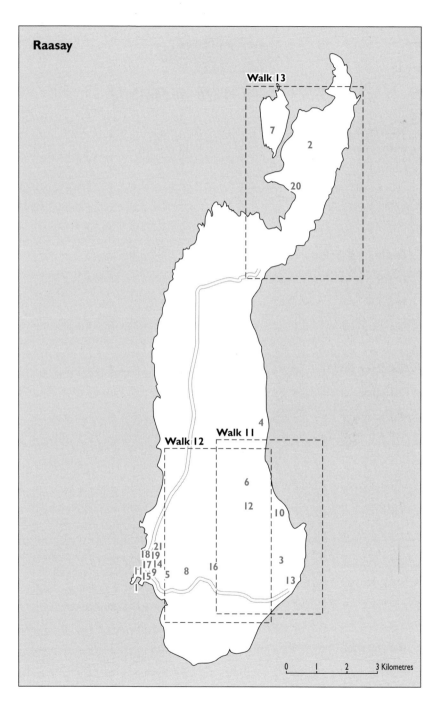

Raasay

Walk 13

7

2

20

Walk 11

Walk 12

4

6

12

10

21
18 19
17 14
9
15
11
5 8 16

3

13

1

0   1   2   3 Kilometres

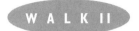

East Coast Walk to Hallaig

Main interest and sights	Beautiful woods, a variety of flowers and other wildlife on a wonderful section of coast. Visit to a deserted township: North Fearns (13) Beinn na' Leac (3) Druim an Aonaich (4) Hallaig (10)
Route	Circular
Grade	Moderate
Map	OS Landranger sheet 24 or 32
Starting point	Picnic spot at highest point of road east of Inverarish, GR 579359
Finishing point	As above
Distance	7 km/4^1/$_4$ mi (3^1/$_2$ hours)
Paths and terrain	A grassy track later becomes a path of deteriorating quality. Effectively unpathed and quite rough ground heading back from Hallaig with some gradient on this section. No navigational problems, however
Options	(a) The easiest, although not the speediest, return from Hallaig is back along the coast the way you came (easy/moderate, 3^3/$_4$ hours) (b) Energetic walkers might wish to explore farther north, below the fascinating escarpment landscapes of Druim an Aonaich. It is possible to walk all the way through to Brochel (moderate/strenuous, 5^1/$_2$ hours)
Nearby walks	Walk 12 and Short Walk 12
Refreshments	None en route; nearest at Inverarish

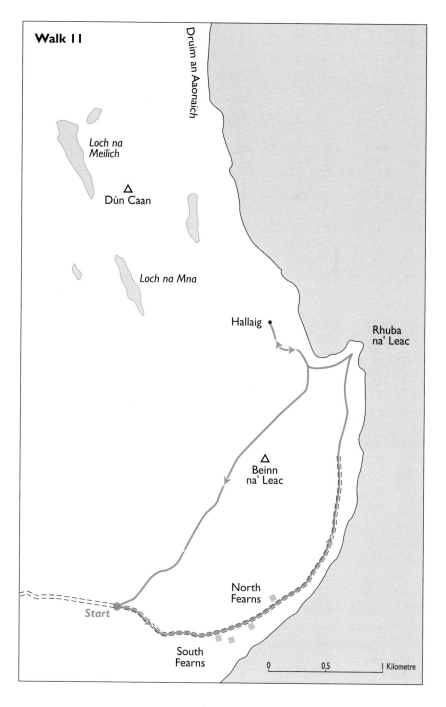

Walk 11

Druim an Aaonaich

Loch na
Meilich

△
Dùn Caan

Loch na Mna

Hallaig

Rhuba
na' Leac

△
Beinn
na' Leac

North
Fearns

Start

South
Fearns

0   0.5   1 Kilometre

This is a walk for lovers of coastal scenery, geology and wildlife, and by venturing as far as the deserted township of Hallaig, one also encounters evidence of what was once a thriving island community. At the right time of year there is a unique variety of wild flowers on display and a real chance of spotting an eagle.

Make your way down from the picnic spot at the highest point of the road east of Inverarish. The views to the island of Scalpay, the uninhabited Crowlin Islands and the Isle of Skye are magnificent. At **North Fearns** (13), the road bears north, passing crofts and the ruins of old cottages, before the tarmac road ends at the last habitable cottage.

From the road end, continue along the coast on a grassy track beneath the birch trees that spread out in a ribbon across the east-facing lower slopes of **Beinn na' Leac** (3). In springtime, many flowers bring colour to the woodland floor. There are wood anemones and bluebells and, growing on carpets of moss that cover the low walls beside the path, primroses and ferns. Among the animal life there are one or two oddities, including a unique species of bank vole, darker and twice the weight of the mainland vole and possibly related to a Scandinavian species. It is also noteworthy that Raasay is the only island in the Hebrides where there is any chance of seeing pine martens.

Following a gently rising path above the sea, go beyond a recent landslide. Be sure to keep to the path, avoiding the impenetrable swathes of bracken. After passing a walled enclosure, continue north to the headland of Rubha na' Leac.

Beside the path immediately above the headland, at GR 598379, stands a cairn commemorating the residents of Hallaig. This is a wonderful place to pause a while to take in the superb coastal scenery and imagine the people who once farmed these cliffs. The east coast escarpment of **Druim an Aonaich** (4) extends for many kilometres farther north, tempting more adventurous walkers into further exploration (see Options). Behind the escarpment rises the unmistakable profile of Dùn Caan (Walk 12) while the attractive bay below is said to be good for fossil hunting. The surrounding woods contain a lovely mix of birch, willow and rowan trees, with rare flora including alpines, saxifrages and orchids.

From the cairn walk west, bearing northwest, crossing a burn on descent. Having reached the other side, enter the large drystone enclosure that once housed the residents of **Hallaig** (10) ($1^3/_4$ hours). The best-preserved section of this pre-clearance township is found among the crumbling walls of the deserted cottages at the top, south, corner of the enclosure. Raasay-born Gaelic poet Sorley MacLean immortalised Hallaig in his poem of the same name, testimony to sad times of poverty and forced emigration in the early

1800s. The situation was exacerbated during the potato famines of the 1830s, despite the laird, MacLeod of Raasay, exhausting his fortune to help the islanders. Eventually he was forced to emigrate himself. Neglect inevitably followed, and the way was left open for a Mr MacFarlane, in 1893, to establish an uncompromisingly strict branch of the Free Church, one that is still followed on Raasay today.

Leave Hallaig by going back across the burn then strike off right up a broad heather-covered ridge towards Beinn na' Leac. Once below the crags of that hill, try to find the trace of a path rising southwest. It can be difficult to follow in places and the terrain is rough, but attempt to keep to a course along the crest of a heather-covered bank wherever possible. The advantages of persevering through territory that has been little trodden include encounters with wildlife that favour seclusion, such as a golden eagles, frequently seen below Beinn na' Leac.

On gaining the crest of the pass at 260 m/853 ft, descend the left bank of a burn. Continue southwest through a narrowing gap and ford the burn on your right at a suitable crossing point. From there, simply descend the unpathed hill slope, making a beeline for the picnic table by the road.

Dùn Caan

Main interest and sights	Evidence of an industrial past and one of the most breathtaking views in the Hebrides: Raasay Iron Mine (16) Loch na Mna (12) Dùn Caan (6)
Route	Linear
Grade	Moderate/strenuous
Map	OS Landranger sheet 24 or 32
Starting point	FC parking place on edge of Raasay Forest by disused mine workings, GR 564365
Finishing point	As above
Distance	9 km/5$^1/_2$ mi (3$^3/_4$ hours)
Paths and terrain	Begins with good forestry track but path thereafter is, in many places, wet, traversing boggy ground. Some walking over rocky outcrops and a steep final push up to Dùn Caan
Options	(a) A shorter return walk (or descent) to/from the summit of Dùn Caan is possible by the wet path rising from Loch Eadar da Bhaile, on the island road to the northwest (moderate, 3 hours)
	(b) A most adventurous route to and from the summit is via Hallaig (reached by Walk 11), Loch a' Chadha-chàrnaich and Dùn Caan's bouldery southeast slope (moderate/strenuous, up to 5$^3/_4$ hours depending on your route of return)
Nearby walks	Walk 11 and Short Walk 12
Refreshments	None en route; nearest at Inverarish.

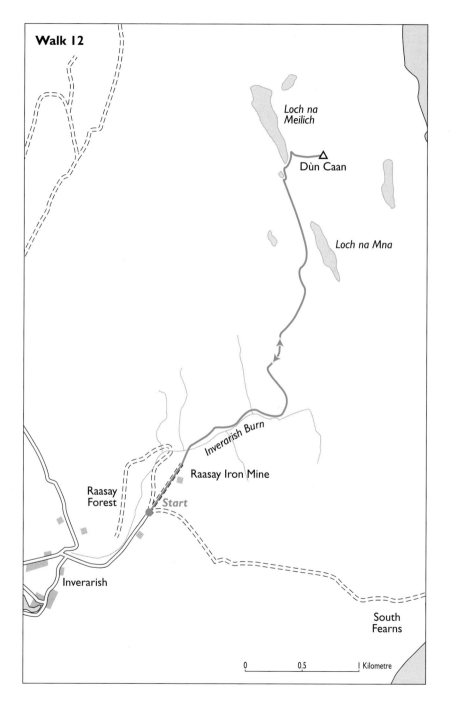

Walk 12

Loch na
Meilich

△
Dùn Caan

Loch na Mna

Inverarish Burn

Raasay Iron Mine

Raasay
Forest

Start

Inverarish

South
Fearns

0   0.5   I Kilometre

Resembling a big heel on an upturned shoe, the distinctive flat-topped hill of **Dùn Caan** (6) is the definitive landmark of Raasay and its highest point. The view is worthy of inspiring the celebration that James Boswell enjoyed when he reached the summit: 'We mounted up to the top of Dun-caan, where we sat down, ate cold mutton and bread and cheese and drank brandy punch. Then we had a Highland song . . . then we danced a reel.'

Begin at the forest edge in the vicinity of the crumbling buildings and abandoned workings of Raasay's disused **Iron Mine** (16). It was developed early in the twentieth century by William Baird & Co. Operational from just before to just after the First World War, its veins of ore were worked by German prisoners of war. Several kilometres of narrow gauge railway linked the mine with the pier at East Suisnish and the old track bed is still visible today.

Cross the timber bridge over the burn and walk north by the edge of Raasay Forest. At the second footbridge, follow the sign for the path on the right, 'Dùn Caan – unmarked path'. Follow the Inverarish Burn upstream along a typically wet path that climbs steadily over open moorland.

You will come to a route-marking cairn after about an hour or so. Pass a second such cairn that lies immediately due north and head for Dùn Caan, farther north still but now tantalisingly close. Having made it above an east-facing escarpment, one has the opportunity to look down on **Loch na Mna** (12), which means 'Loch of the Woman', so named from times when a water creature from the loch frequently devoured the beautiful women of the island. Not surprisingly, there is also a druid explanation for the name: the loch is said to have once been a place where virgins were sacrificed.

Continue north along the top of the rock face to a tiny lochan. Drop down steeply for about 25 m/80 ft to reach the shore of Loch na Meilich. This is a public water supply for the island so swimming is not allowed.

From the loch a path that zigzags steeply up the west side of Dùn Caan to the summit of the hill ($1^3/_4$ hours) will leave you breathless but exuberant. A trig pillar sits on the edge of the flat, grassy table-top and overlooks the steep east face of Dùn Caan as well as Loch a' Chadha-chàrnaich and the beautiful coast at Hallaig (Walk 11). Yet more enchanting are the distant vistas: the Skye Cuillin to the south and southwest and the Torridons, the Applecross hills and the Knoydart mountains across on the mainland, beyond the Inner Sound.

Few perches in Scotland can match the delight of the panorama from Dùn Caan, yet the hill may be special in less obvious ways. Another druidic claim for Raasay is that Dùn Caan is linked to Skye's Old Man of Storr (Walk 9) by a ley line (a line of natural earth energy) although such invisible connections between prominent landmarks are, apparently, commonplace and may be the lines of prehistoric tracks. Return to Raasay Forest the same way.

Torran Woods and the North

Main interest and sights	Delightful scrub woodland and fine views: Torran woods (20) Eilean Fladday (7) Beinn na h-Iolaire (2)
Route	Circular
Grade	Easy/moderate
Map	OS Landranger sheet 24
Starting point	North end of the island road at Arnish, GR 594480
Finishing point	As above
Distance	6.8 km/4^1/$_4$ mi (2^3/$_4$ hours)
Paths and terrain	Good tracks and mostly well-defined paths. Steep on the climb from the shore above Caol Fladda and wet underfoot in places. Walking boots recommended
Options	There are a couple of straightforward options for extending this walk: (a) From Beinn na h-Iolaire descend east to the ruined shielings by the shore facing Applecross. Remember you will have to climb back up, which means clocking up over 500 m/1,640 ft of ascent in total (moderate, 3^3/$_4$ hours) (b) You can walk out to the northern extremity of Raasay (and even on to Eilean Tigh if the tide is out) by the path passing the old shielings of An Caol (moderate, 5 hours)
Nearby walks	None; nearest is Short Walk 12
Refreshments	None en route; nearest at Inverarish

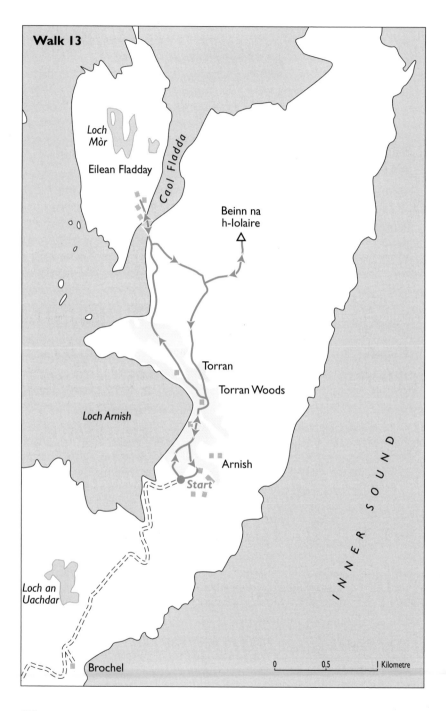

Walk 13

Loch Mòr

Eilean Fladday

Caol Fladda

Beinn na h-Iolaire
△

Torran

Torran Woods

Loch Arnish

Arnish

Start

I N N E R   S O U N D

Loch an Uachdar

Brochel

0   0.5   1 Kilometre

Whereas the southern part of Raasay is composed primarily of Torridonian sandstone, the north of the island is of Archaean gneiss. Given this distribution, the landscapes at either end of the island have quite different characters. The scrub-like woodland at Torran has a sparse but very wild feel to it, an atmosphere that contrasts with the lush garden-like welcome from the trees in the vicinity of Clachan (Short Walk 12). This walk ventures through the **Torran woods** (20) towards a tiny tidal island and then climbs to a superb viewpoint.

First take a quick look at the picturesque ruins of the sixteenth-century castle at Brochel, located 2.5 km/1¹/₂ mi before the road end. The castle was built by the first laird of Raasay, Calum MacGillichalium (of the MacLeods of Lewis). It remained a MacLeod stronghold for just over 100 years, until abandoned in favour of more fertile lands at Clachan. There is also a commemorative cairn by the road, at GR 585466, to honour the amazing feat of Calum MacLeod. In 1966, with a pick, shovel and wheelbarrow, he single-handedly constructed this section of road between Brochel and Arnish, in despair at the council's refusal to upgrade the existing path. Such tales of defiance and determination are not untypical in the islands; rather, they characterise the resourcefulness and resilience of the Hebridean.

From the end of the road, pursue a track signposted 'Torran Fladda'. It dips down to the left, passing through the delightful birch scrub of the Torran woodland, which extends around the bay of Loch Arnish. Go past two fishing cottages, but then after a third (20 minutes), the track becomes a wet path. There was a school here at Torran until 1960.

On emerging above the birch trees, one has a clearer view of Loch Arnish and, inevitably, its salmon cages. The path descends along a delightful coastal stretch to the base of Piper's Cliff, at the east shore of a narrow channel of water known as Caol Fladda. This can be crossed at low tide via a causeway to visit the little island of **Eilean Fladday** (7), which was once inhabited by four families who had their own school but whose houses are now holiday homes. Walk back up the way you came for a short distance to gain the path that forks left for a climb that is short but steep. Soon you are up into a rugged landscape characterised by heather and gneiss outcrops.

Bear left at a cairn marking the joining of paths (alternatively, turn right if you wish to shorten the walk). Continue up over the moorland, where the flowers that manage to grow are typical of nutrient-poor soils and include butterwort and bird's-foot trefoil. At the highest point of the path, strike off left, crossing easy terrain to the trig pillar on **Beinn na h-Iolaire** (2) (1¹/₂ hours). The top of this hill commands spectacular views in every direction. Across the Sound of Raasay are the Trotternish Ridge and the Cuillin of

Skye; to the east, across the Inner Sound, you can gaze upon a panorama of the hills of Applecross. The view south extends over much of the rest of Raasay, with conspicuous Dùn Caan (Walk 12) rising above everything else.

Walk back to the junction of paths by the cairn you passed earlier and continue straight on. The path then skirts below an impressive curve of gneiss cliffs. Dùn Caan is ahead as you descend through birch and hazel scrub to regain the track at Torran. The final leg of the return can be varied slightly by walking off to the left through a grassy gap in the trees and gaining the Arnish track. This then leads down to join the road.

Raasay House, Raasay

Short Walk

12 RAASAY HOUSE AND FOREST (2 HOURS; OSLR MAP 24)

There are many points of interest close to Raasay House and in the surrounding forest. Most of the important architectural and archaeological sites on the island are located in this beautiful, garden-like corner of the island. They can all be visited within a couple of hours.

Begin the walk at **The Battery** (1) (GR 546363), at the north end of Churchton Bay. Although now only one remains, in 1807 five cannon were placed here on a rocky knoll by the MacLeods. By the pier are two stone mermaids, their gazes fixed on Skye. They were commissioned by the nineteenth-century laird John MacLeod after his steward returned from Italy on a mission to collect artefacts. MacLeod never took to the busty maidens so had them sited well away from the house, condemned to serve as sentinels over the Narrows of Raasay. Of greater age is a cross carving of Pictish origins, the trace of which is just visible on a rock face beside the boathouse.

Follow the track up to **Raasay House** (15), a very salubrious residence until John MacLeod was forced to sell in 1843. It remains a listed building but, having long since relinquished its grandeur, now serves as an outdoor centre. The **Heritage Museum** (11) is located in the west wing and displays all kinds of fascinating memorabilia of Raasay through the ages (contact Margaret Moodie, telephone 01478 660295). Leave Raasay House by the east drive, passing the **Fountain Pond** (9) on the right. The fountain, now in overgrown surroundings, can be switched on if you want to see it working.

Turn left at the road to visit **St Moluag's Chapel** (18), an evocative thirteenth-century ruin on consecrated ground with much of its fine masonry still intact. It was constructed as a monument to St Moluag, the Irish missionary. A little farther along the lane, in the trees on the right, can be seen an interesting seventh-century **Pictish Stone** (14), an incised Ogam (Pictish writing) stone.

A few metres beyond the Pictish Stone, leave the road for a FC path on the right, for 'Temptation Hill Trail'. This leads up to **Temptation Hill** (19) – so magnificent was the view from it that it tempted a MacLeod of Lewis to become the island's owner. From a gravestone on the hill, 'In loving memory of darling Kit', follow waymarkers, turning right at a forestry track and then right again at a tarmac lane. From the south side of Loch' Mhuilin, go up along a path on the left then turn right at Trail markers. Walk on through the conifers to reach **Dùn Borodale** (5) broch, another relic of the Picts on Raasay, which still has part of its walls and galleries remaining.

Continue on the Temptation Hill Trail, going down past the Free Church to the junction of Burma Road with the main island road at Inverarish. The walk along the road towards Churchton Bay is especially delightful in early summer when the rhododendrons and fuchsias are in bloom.

On the opposite side of the road from the Isle of Raasay Hotel, a gap in the wall gives access to the recently discovered **Uamhna Ramh Souterrain** (21). The builders of this fascinating underground dwelling house and passageway utilised a natural fissure in the rock and constructed a roof with stone lintels. This souterrain is within a craggy rhododendron-covered mound and you can walk right through it. Thought to be more than 2,000 years old, its original purpose is something of a mystery although it was possibly a storehouse or may even have had some religious significance. Uamhna Ramh means 'cave of the oars' as in more recent times it is known that the oars of local galleys were hidden there to disguise the evidence of smuggling. Bonnie Prince Charlie was smuggled to Raasay after the Battle of Culloden, the islanders rowing him over from Skye as it was being searched. The Protestant MacLeods of Raasay, unlike their relatives on Lewis and Skye, supported the Jacobites and the Prince was hidden on the island until he could be successfully smuggled over to Loch Broom where he was rescued by a French ship.

Close to the hotel, the old **Stable buildings** (17) of Raasay House are of architectural interest. Of particular note is the clock tower, the clock of which stopped one day in 1914 when 36 Raasay men assembled here to go to war: only 14 returned. From here, follow the road towards the shore overlooking the Narrows, returning to the pier at Clachan.

St Moluag's Chapel, Raasay

Barra and Vatersay

Everyone is made to feel welcome on Barra, the 'perfect island' at the southern tip of the Long Isle. The Long Isle, or Outer Hebrides to give this outlying group of islands their better-known name, is a 200 km/125 mi-long chain of archipelagos, a billion-year old backbone of ancient rock flexing itself defiantly against the Atlantic. Another explanation for the existence of the Long Isle is that the islands are in fact the bones of a nine-headed giant, his skeleton protruding above the waves. Legend has it that the giant was slain by a young man from Skye, who cut off eight heads and stabbed him in the heart in revenge for devouring his betrothed, for the giant had a keen appetite for young women. From above you can still make out the outline of his bones – the Butt of Lewis is said to be the giant's ninth head and, in the far south, the cliffs of Berneray are the soles of his feet.

A tough, severe though undeniably beautiful environment, the Outer Hebrides are inhabited by a people as resilient as the wind-lashed and weather-beaten Lewisian gneiss that constitutes the bedrock of the far northwest of Scotland. The people of the Long Isle are typified as being reserved, with an outward character frequently described as 'dour'. And yet, against the odds perhaps, Barra folk are a positively friendly and joyful lot. It is a place you will soon come to feel at ease in, more so if you can attempt some Gaelic or, better still, play the fiddle.

Castlebay (10), the capital, was once a busy herring port, although, as elsewhere, the industry has long since declined. In Barra's principal township today, a lively yet relaxing air pervades, an atmosphere that reflects not only the outlook of its inhabitants but also the warmth extended to its visitors. Occupying its own isolated lump of rock in the sea is fifteenth-century **Kisimul Castle** (24), ancestral home of the Clan MacNeil. Kisimul is a beautiful fortress when seen from the approaching ferry, where the backdrop is one of hills. A distinctly Scottish scene, except that, unlike their loftier Highland cousins, Barra's hills are agreeably free of persistent rain clouds.

Treeless and barren it may be, but there is nothing too austere or threatening about the island. Barra is just perfect: small enough to allow one to feel the proximity of the sea and to explore on foot in a few days, yet large enough in land area and in character to never become too familiar. Barra is an enchanting place, nominated in 1985 for an International Island Award.

If hills are not quite your thing, there is much more to discover on huge, empty, pale, shell-sand beaches, among spectacular wild summer flowers, in observing rare birds, in seeking out fascinating archaeological remains, or simply plane spotting at the most unusual of airports, or revisiting *Whisky Galore*.

MAIN SETTLEMENTS
Castlebay is the principal township of Barra and has much of the island's hotel and B&B accommodation. Close to the pier and overlooking Kisimul Castle is the tourist information office. Castlebay has shops, hotel bars, cafés, a school and the island's hospital, bank and main post office. Most other essential services are to be found here. There are sizeable crofting and fishing communities also at Earsary, Eoligarry, Bayherivagh, Borve and on Vatersay, most with at least a post office.

ACCESS
The Cal Mac vehicle and passenger ferry sails from Oban four to five times per week, with a crossing time of about five hours. This same ferry also connects with Lochboisdale (South Uist) in both directions. From Eoligarry, a private passenger ferry operates to and from Ludag on South Uist, sometimes calling at Eriskay (telephone 01878 720238).

A British Airways Twin Otter plane operates from Barra Airport, the big beach on Cockle Strand, with daily connecting flights to Glasgow, Stornoway and Benbecula.

ACCOMMODATION
The Castlebay Hotel and the Craigard Hotel are both at Castlebay while the Isle of Barra Hotel overlooks Tangasdale Beach on the west coast. There are also about a dozen B&Bs scattered across the island and about the same number of self-catering options. No hostel or bunkhouse accommodation is currently available.

PUBLIC TRANSPORT
A bus service (W32) operates six or seven times per day on circuits around the island on the A888 from Castlebay, a route that also includes Eoligarry and the airport. There is also a bus (W33) about three times per day to Vatersay from Castlebay. A postbus between Castlebay and Eoligarry serves Barra daily although journeys are much longer. There are no Sunday services on any route.

Both car hire and bicycle hire is possible at Castlebay.

ORDNANCE SURVEY LANDRANGER MAPS
Landranger Sheet 31 covers all of Barra and Vatersay.

MAIN PLACES OF INTEREST
Allt Chrysal antiquities (1) Walk 15
'Annie Jane' monument (2) Walk 14
Barra Heritage Centre (3) Local history, cultural activities and restaurant in Castlebay
Beinn Mhartainn (4) Walk 16
Ben Eoligarry (5) Walk 17
Ben Erival (6) Short Walk 14
Ben Tangaval (7) Walk 15
Bhatarsaigh Standing Stone (8) Walk 14
Borve Point (9) Short Walk 13
Castlebay (10) Walk 16
Cille Bharra (11) Walk 17
Cockle Strand (12) Walk 17 and Short Walk 14
Craigston Museum (13) Walk 16
Doirlinn Head (14) Walk 15
Dùn Bharpa (15) Walk 16
Dùn Bhatarsaigh (16) Walk 14
Dùn Chuidhir (17) Iron Age broch remains close to A888 at Grein, GR 664034
Dùn Mhic Léoid (18) Walk 16
Dunollie Golf Course (19) Most westerly golf club in the UK; home of Barra Golf Club
Dùn Scurrival (20) Walk 17
Eoligarry (21) Walk 17 and Short Walk 14
Eorasdail (22) Walk 14
Heaval (23) Walk 16
Kisimul Castle (24) Walk 16
'Our Lady of the Sea' statue (25) Walk 16
Sound of Vatersay (26) Walk 15
West Beach and Vatersay Bay (27) Walk 14

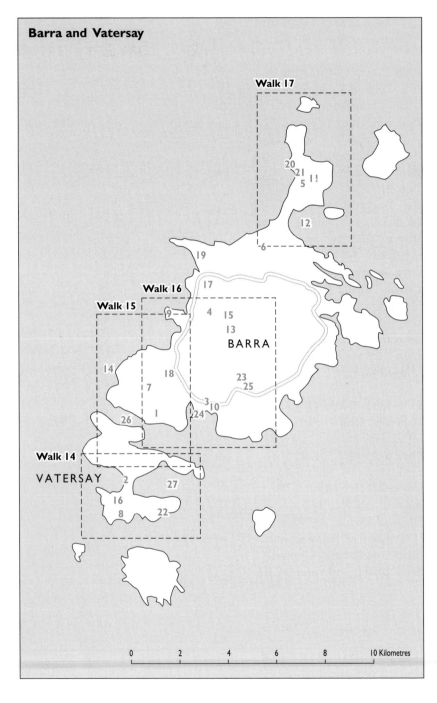

Barra and Vatersay

Walk 17

BARRA

Walk 16

Walk 15

VATERSAY

Walk 14

0   2   4   6   8   10 Kilometres

Vatersay

Main interest and sights	Glorious Hebridean beaches. A treat for nature lovers, and for those seeking 'heritage': West Beach and Vatersay Bay (27) 'Annie Jane' monument (2) Dùn Bhatarsaigh (16) Bhatarsaigh Standing Stone (8) Eorasdail (22)
Route	Circular
Grade	Easy/moderate
Map	OS Landranger sheet 31
Starting point	Vatersay Bay; car park at GR 633953
Finishing point	As above
Distance	6.4 km/4 mi ($2^3/_4$ hours)
Paths and terrain	Effectively unpathed but easy terrain with just a few wet patches and little gradient
Options	The highest point of Vatersay is the hill of the northern half of the island, Heishival (Theseabhal) Mòr, from which there are fine views of the beaches and of the Sounds of Sandray and of Barra. Climbing it from Vatersay Bay is an easy addition to the route (moderate, $4^1/_2$ hours)
Nearby walks	Walk 15
Refreshments	None en route; nearest at Castlebay on Barra

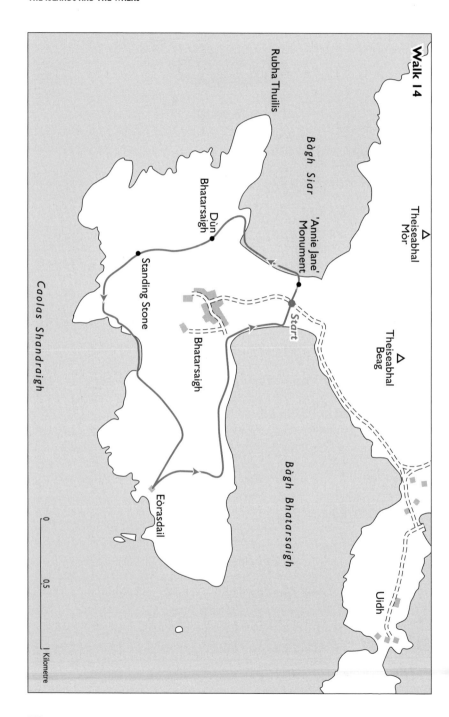

Walk 14

Theiseabhal
Mòr △

Theiseabhal
Beag △

Rubha Thuilis

Bàgh Siar

'Annie Jane'
Monument

Dùn
Bhatarsaigh

Standing Stone

Bhatarsaigh

Start

Caolas Shandraigh

Bàgh Bhatarsaigh

Eòrasdail

Uidh

0   0.5   1 Kilometre

Vatersay was, until late in the last century, a separate island in its own right. However, a causeway opened in 1990 has now joined it to Barra. With the Sound of Vatersay effectively blocked, Castlebay enjoys even greater protection from Atlantic seas. But Vatersay is, for its established crofting community at least, far more than just Barra's storm buffer.

This ramble around Vatersay's southern half is a walk that has a bit of everything that is typically of the Hebrides, and you can see it all in a morning or an afternoon.

The car park is at the side of the road at the point marked 'Heritage Trail' on up-to-date OS maps. For much of the way, the walk is waymarked and begins on the narrow neck of dunes between the glorious sands of **Vatersay Bay (Bàgh Bhatarsaigh)** and **West Beach (Bàgh Siar)** (27). A short stroll over the dunes leads to a prominent granite obelisk, the **'Annie Jane' monument** (2). It marks the burial site of emigrants drowned when, on 28 September 1853, the *Annie Jane* was tragically shipwrecked in the bay. An inscription reads 'And the sea gave up her dead that were in it'.

Drop down over the dunes and walk to the south end of West Beach, then go up to post '2' and over a stile. Once above the bay, you can expect vivid and colourful displays of summer machair flowers such as poppies and other flora typical of the disturbed areas of worked-potato patches (see page 26). Bear west to reach post '3', then head south again up to **Dùn Bhatarsaigh** (16). The dun occupies a prominent hilltop site although little remains of the original Iron Age construction, its stones having been utilised in later buildings. From here, the ruins of Bhatarsaigh House can be seen in front of the main village. Follow a grassy path south to a stile over a fence and then traverse a wetter area where yellow flag and northern marsh orchid thrive. Between May and August you may hear corncrakes in the vicinity.

At marker post '8', bear right and walk south-southwest, following an overgrown wall, towards a **Standing Stone** (8) silhouetted against the skyline. This Bronze Age relic, its original purpose a mystery, has since become a gatepost. From here, walk down towards the shore but without going quite as far. This avoids the obstacle of a deep inlet on bearing east.

South Beach (Bàgh a' Deas) is favoured by cattle with an eye for beauty; on a calm, clear day this secluded suntrap is idyllic. As it is well off the beaten track, the bay is a paradise you are unlikely to have to share with two-legged beasts. A stile over fencing gives access to its pristine sands and turquoise waters.

From the east end of the bay, follow further marker posts up away from the beach, traversing machair and grass to reach post '11'. This is the point to make a brief diversion, if you wish, to visit the ruins of **Eorasdail** (22) to the south. Most of the walls of the roofless cottages are still intact, as Eorasdail was inhabited as late as the 1970s. The township was established after the Bhatarsaigh Land Raids in 1909. At that time, desperate crofters from Barra and Sandray laid claim to some land on Vatersay as a simple matter of survival. The men became known as the Vatersay Raiders and, despite imprisonment (or perhaps because of it), attained hero-like status.

Walk north from Eorosdail towards the opposite shore, over the pass between Beinn Chuidhir and Am Meall. Turn left from above a small jetty and simply follow the bay around to the northeast of the present-day township where most of the population of Vatersay resides.

Statue of 'Our Lady of the Sea', on Sheabhal, Barra

Barra Airport

Deas Bay, Vatersay, Barra

Ormacleit Castle and farm, South Uist

Machair, South Uist

Pobull Fhinn Stone circle, North Uist

Marrum grass and dunes, North Uist

Teampall na h-Uidhe, Toe Head, South Harris

'The Bays' from the Golden Road, Harris

Dun Carloway broch, Lewis

Standing Stones, Callanish, Lewis

Callanish, Lewis

The Great Stack, Handa

W A L K 15

Beinn Tangaval and the Sound of Vatersay

Main interest and sights	Recently discovered archaeological remains, grand views and fascinating coastal features. Ornithological interest too: Allt Chrysal antiquities (1) Ben Tangaval (Beinn Tangabhal) (7) Doirlinn Head (Rubha na Doirlinn) (14) Sound of Vatersay (Caolas Bhatarsaigh) (26)
Route	Circular
Grade	Moderate/strenuous
Map	OS Landranger sheet 31
Starting point	400 m/$^1/_4$ mi east of Vatersay causeway, GR 643977
Finishing point	As above
Distance	7.6 km/4$^3/_4$ mi (4 hours)
Paths and terrain	No established paths to follow, with quite rough and steep terrain. Potential navigational errors descending Ben Tangaval.
Options	(a) If the hill is in mist, limit the walk to the coastal section as far as Doirlinn Head and go back to the causeway the same way (moderate, 3$^1/_2$ hours) (b) Ben Tangaval can also be climbed from the north, from Tangasdal via Dùn Ban, then down the southeast side and back by the road (moderate, 3$^3/_4$ hours)
Nearby walks	Walk 14 and 16 and Short Walk 13
Refreshments	None en route; nearest are Castlebay shops and bars and the hotel at Halaman Bay (Bàgh Thalaman)

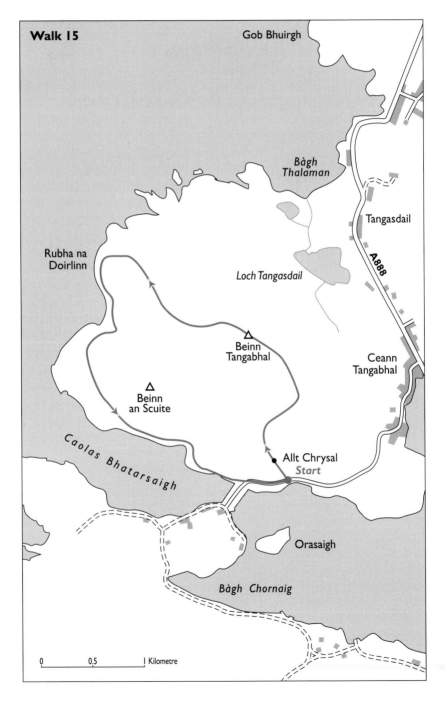

Walk 15

Gob Bhuirgh

Bàgh Thalaman

Tangasdail

A888

Loch Tangasdail

Rubha na Doirlinn

△ Beinn Tangabhal

Ceann Tangabhal

△ Beinn an Scuite

Caolas Bhatarsaigh

Allt Chrysal
Start

Orasaigh

Bàgh Chornaig

0   0.5   1 Kilometre

In contrast to the level sweeping beaches of pale shell sand to the north, the untamed southwest corner of the island is noticeably more rugged. The Tangaval peninsula is out on a limb, almost completely encircled by an energetic sea, a wild and exposed extremity where wave-smashed cliffs butt against the full force of the Atlantic. But the walk begins in a more peaceful setting, among recently discovered archaeological remains.

From the north side of the road, just east of the Vatersay causeway, go through a metal gate and head up the shallow valley of the burn. Almost at once, you will come upon the site where excavation of **Allt Chrysal** (1) is taking place. The site was first unearthed in 1990, during the archaeological survey on Ben Tangaval that preceded the building of the Vatersay causeway and its approach road. Evidence has been uncovered of Neolithic settlers here about 4,500 years ago, including a rectangular oven showing layers of burnt clay. As each occupation apparently reused the materials utilised by their predecessors, the picture is not complete, but it is known that there have been at least six phases of human occupation since then. Drinking beakers have been found, as have the remains of small circular stone-built huts. A later Iron Age farmhouse and an eighteenth-century farm have also been identified.

Continue through heather up along the course of the burn. At the top of the valley, bear right and northeast, ascending the open hill to a cairn-marked summit at 230 m/755 ft. You will pass close to a tiny lochan along the way, a secluded pool of water where I once was greeted by the magnificent sight of a pair of red-throated divers. Turn northwest from the cairn and continue the ascent to the very top of **Ben Tangaval** (7) (1¹/₄ hours). The best views are from the edges of this rocky summit plateau, far-reaching in every direction, over to Barra's beautiful west coast beaches as well as to those of Vatersay.

About 250 m farther northwest of the summit proper, there is a large cairn that marks the spot for descending a broad ridge. First head west, then bear north-northwest where the ridge becomes more defined. At the last cairn lower down, an easily seen pile of stones out on a promontory, again turn west and descend to the cliff edge. At this point go left and follow the cliff top southwards, traversing short turf and barren outcrops of gneiss.

The cliff scenery around **Doirlinn Head** (14) is truly spectacular. There is a sea-worn arch at the Head, best viewed by looking back from the south. The place is far enough away from humanity to attract eagles and peregrine falcons. Follow the curve around a rocky bay, and then a miniature gorge must be overcome before the climb up to a cairn at GR 623988. From here, gradually veer eastwards, dropping down to just above the shoreline in the **Sound of Vatersay** (26). As you approach the causeway, look out for seals basking on the rocks. Cross the sheep-fencing where there is no barbed wire, at the corner by the road.

W A L K 16

Castlebay and the Big Hills

Main interest and sights	Begins from a beautiful sheltered bay followed by an ascent of Barra's highest hills: Castlebay (10) Kisimul Castle (24) Heaval (Sheabhal) (23) 'Our Lady of the Sea' (25) Dùn Bharpa (15) Beinn Mhartainn (4) Craigston Museum (13) Dùn Mhic Lèoid (18)
Route	Circular
Grade	Moderate/strenuous
Map	OS Landranger sheet 31
Starting point	Castlebay Hotel, GR 666983
Finishing point	As above
Distance	13.3 km/8^{1}/$_{4}$ mi (5^{1}/$_{2}$ hours)
Paths and terrain	Unpathed grassy hill slopes with fairly well-defined ridge between summits. A few steep gradients and about 600 m/2,000 ft of ascent but no real difficulties. Long return on tarmac
Options	(a) Significantly shorter circuits are possible by coming off the east sides of Heaval or Hartaval at any convenient point, meeting the A888 south of Earsairidh (b) For even longer excursions, walk out to Beinn Mhartainn or combine with Short Walk 13 or Short Walk 14
Nearby walks	Walk 15 and Short Walks 13 and 14
Refreshments	Shops, hotel and bars in Castlebay and hotel at Halaman Bay (Tangasdal)

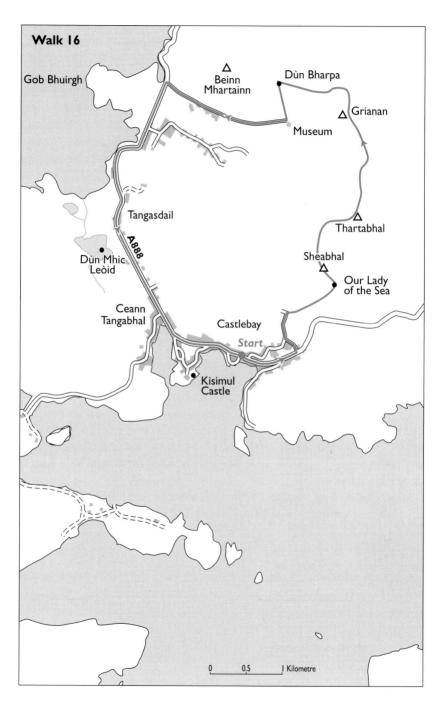

Walk 16

Gob Bhuirgh

Beinn Mhartainn

Dùn Bharpa

Grianan

Museum

Tangasdail

A888

Dùn Mhic Leòid

Thartabhal

Sheabhal

Our Lady of the Sea

Ceann Tangabhal

Castlebay

Start

Kisimul Castle

0   0.5   1 Kilometre

The walk begins in **Castlebay** (10), one of the most attractive harbours in the Outer Hebrides. **Kisimul Castle** (24), which dominates the bay, is the home of the present owner of Barra, Ian MacNeil. The MacNeils have always been a very proud family. One famous story tells of how, when one particular MacNeil had finished dinner, he had his piper play from the castle ramparts and proclaim to the four corners of the world, 'The MacNeil has dined. The other potentates of the earth may now dine.'

Climbing north, the route follows the south to north line of the island's highest summits, visiting a couple of historical sites before passing close to the beaches on the west coast, via a return along the main island road.

First make for a gate in the fence at Gleann, on the footpath at the back of the houses on the east side of Castlebay. This allows access to **Heaval** (23) (Sheabhal), the high hill that so dominates the bay. The climb on its south side is quite steep, pathless but straightforward. Aiming for a point just below and to the right of the summit will soon find you at **Our Lady of the Sea** (25), a striking white marble statue and symbol of the islanders' resolutely Catholic faith. Maternal and defiant, Madonna with Child gazes eastwards, ever vigilant, towards Rum and the mainland.

One must summon a little more energy to reach the trig pillar on the summit of Heaval, at 383 m/1,203 ft the highest place in the Barra Isles. Beyond Castlebay, the uninhabited seabird islands of the far south can be seen, including Pabbay, Mingulay and Berneray. To the northwest, on a very distant horizon, lie Scotland's remotest islands, those of St Kilda.

From Heaval, the walk continues north along a well-defined grassy ridge and over further cairn-marked summits as far as Greanan (Grianan). The cool breeze that blows almost constantly over the hills of Barra can be a positive tonic in summer, with the added benefit of keeping midges well out of devouring range.

Having made it to Greanan (2^1/$_2$ hours), you will find it is all downhill (for the body, not the spirit) from here. First descend north, but rather than climb again to the next summit, turn left and walk down to a sheep fence. Follow this around to the left, then go over a stile and continue west to reach the huge pile of stones marking the Neolithic chambered burial cairn of **Dùn Bharpa** (15) (3^1/$_4$ hours). It is an impressive site on the saddle between Grianan and **Beinn Mhartainn** (16), although one is no longer able to enter its chambers. From Dùn Bharpa, continue downhill and south for 500 m/^{1}/$_3$ mi, to the top of the road at Baile na Creige. A restored thatched cottage houses **Craigston Museum** (13), which offers visitors an insight into the past and traditional crofting on Barra.

The return to Castlebay is mostly level, on tarmac, skirting behind the lovely sandy bays on either side of Borve Point (Short Walk 13) and passing a freshwater loch at Tangasdal. Here, below the hill of the same name, stand the ruins of a castle tower on an islet, **Dùn Mhic Lèoid** (18).

Kisimul Castle, Barra

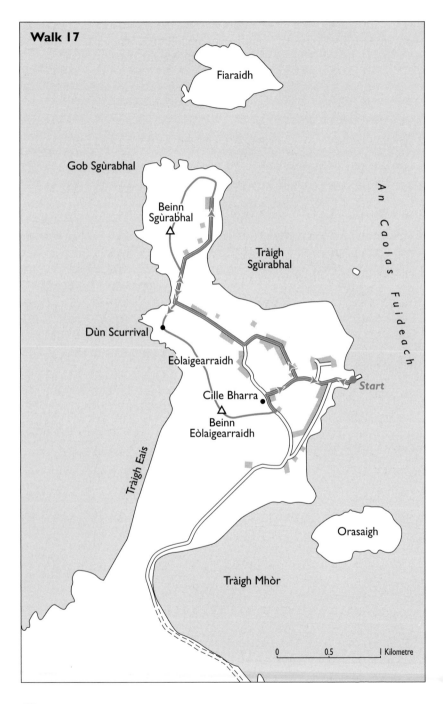

Walk 17

Fiaraidh

Gob Sgùrabhal

Beinn
Sgùrabhal
△

Tràigh
Sgùrabhal

An Caolas Fuideach

Dùn Scurrival

Eòlaigearraidh

Cille Bharra

Beinn
Eòlaigearraidh
△

Start

Tràigh Eais

Orasaigh

Tràigh Mhòr

0   0.5   1 Kilometre

Around Eoligarry (Eòlaigearraidh)

Main interest and sights	Vast empty beaches and an important site of antiquity: Eoligarry (Eòlaigearraidh) (21) Dùn Scurrival (Dun Sgùrabhal) (20) Ben Eoligarry (Beinn Eòlaigearraidh) (5) Big Sand/Cockle Strand (Tràigh Mhòr) (12) Cille Bharra (Cille-bharra) (11)
Route	Circular
Grade	Moderate
Map	OS Landranger sheet 31
Starting point	Eolaigearraidh jetty, GR 713076
Finishing point	As above
Distance	8.5 km/5^1/$_4$ mi (3^1/$_4$ hours)
Paths and terrain	Relatively straightforward terrain up and down the low hills with non-taxing gradients
Options	(a) This is a figure-of-8 circuit so it is easy to omit the section that includes Ben Scurrival (Beinn Sgùrabhal) (easy to moderate, 2^1/$_4$ hours) (b) Wandering over the beautiful sands of Tràigh Sgùrabhal provides a tarmac-free route to Beinn Sgùrabhal at low tide
Nearby walks	Short Walk 14
Refreshments	None en route; nearest at pub at Bagh Shiarabhagh, on A888

The topography of Barra's northern peninsula consists of a slither of grey gneiss surrounded by some of the most magnificent expanses of pale shell sand in the Hebrides. There are easy hills to climb around **Eoligarry** (21) to view the beaches, to observe the machair, to see other islands across the Sound of Barra and to look down upon one of the world's most romantic airports. A visit to Barra's most important ecclesiastical site gives a fascinating historical and religious dimension to a walk of scenic splendour. If you are lucky, you may even catch a sight of the small group of bottlenose dolphins that frequent the Sound.

From the car park by the jetty, walk down the lane and bear right where it forks. Turn right again and follow the tarmac past the crofts of Eoligarry as far as the very end of the road at the northern tip. There is always a wind blowing at Eoligarry so even on the roads there is every possibility of walking across drifts of sand.

Go through a gate at the north end of the road and turn left, passing through three more gates and over a footbridge. An easy pathless climb then leads to the trig pillar on Ben Scurrival (1¼ hours) with a very fine view over a turquoise sea to many other islands. South Uist is just 7 km/4½ mi to the northeast while just across the Sound, beyond the small island of Fuday, is Eriskay. Upon the completion of a connecting causeway with South Uist in 2001, Eriskay has now relinquished its island status. Eriskay was where Bonnie Prince Charlie first landed in Scotland from France but more recently, and more famously, it is where the SS *Politician* ran aground in February 1941. It broke in two and its cargo of whisky sank with it, inspiring the novelist Sir Compton Mackenzie to write his hilarious book *Whisky Galore*. Using locations on Barra, it was later made into one of Ealing Studios' most successful films. Compton Mackenzie had his home at Eoligarry for a time.

Walk on down from Ben Scurrival towards Eoligarry and gain the road at a gate on the left, on the south side of sheep fencing. Leave the road again where it turns left and continue over a stile and southwards up to **Dùn Scurrival** (20) (1¾ hours). It is now merely a tumble of rocks, but there is no doubting the excellence of its defensive position with a marvellous view along the 2 km/1¼ mi strip of shell sand at West Beach (Tràigh Eais).

To reach **Ben Eoligarry** (5) from Dùn Scurrival (2½ hours), follow marker posts southeast for 1 km/²/₃ mi. From this highest point on the walk, **Tràigh Mhòr**, or **Big Sand** (12), is now in full view. This great sweep of beach is commonly known as **Cockle Strand** because in the eighteenth century, during times of famine, cartloads of live cockles were collected every day from here. Big Sands cockles are said to be especially succulent. Cockle Strand has served as Barra Airport since 1935. Today, it is a runway for a Twin

Otter plane to and from Glasgow and Stornoway that can land or take off only at low tide. Also from this hill, the interesting patchwork pattern of the Eoligarry crofts is seen to good effect.

Descend the east side of Ben Eoligarry, for the gate immediately to the right of **Cille Bharra** (11) cemetery and chapel. The church of St Barr, commemorating the saint who converted the islanders to Christianity in the seventh century, dates from the twelfth century. It is one of three ruined chapels and has been re-roofed to protect medieval grave slabs including the replica of a unique Norse stone with runic markings on one side and a Celtic cross on the other. The original stone was discovered in 1865 and is now in the National Museum of Antiquities in Edinburgh. Sir Compton Mackenzie is buried in the cemetery. Another of the chapels at Cille Bharra is thought to be dedicated to another saint, closely connected to Barra, St Brendan. When sailing in the Minch, off Barra, it was he who met Judas Iscariot seated on an iceberg, apparently on his one day off a year from Hell. The seas around Barra have long been of evil repute, which is maybe why Barra has always been more of a lone island than its neighbours to the north, both geographically and in the beliefs of the islanders. One such example concerns the tradition in the Outer Isles of celebrating the September harvest moon as the 'Fair Moon of St Michael's Feast'. Only on Barra is it celebrated as 'Fair Moon of St Barr'.

The jetty car park is back along the lane to the east of Cille Bharra.

Eoligarry, Barra

Short Walks

13 BORVE POINT (UP TO 1 HOUR; OSLR MAP 31)

This gentle stroll explores the machair, the dunes and the beach on the level headland at **Borve Point** (9), immediately north of Halaman Bay (Bagh Thalaman).

Park near the school and the road junction at Baile na Creige (GR 656019). Walk south along the A888 and after 400 m/^{1}/$_4$ mi strike off right. Pursue a grassy track past a standing stone (said to mark the grave of a Norse warrior killed by a Barra man) to reach the old burial ground. From here walk northeast, staying to the left of a transmission mast. Go over a stile to reach the shore and then follow the coast around the south side of a sandy bay. A lovely beach and the dunes behind it are a pleasant distraction before rejoining the road at GR 656023, with the option of continuing farther north, of course.

14 BEN ERIVAL (BEINN EIREABHAL) (1¼ HOURS; OSLR MAP 31)

Ben Erival (6) overlooks **Tràigh Mhòr** (12), Barra's unique airport on the sand. To my mind the view from its summit is unsurpassed on Barra. The island-studded Sound of Barra provides a vivid turquoise backdrop to the vast sweeps of sand of the Eoligarry peninsula, with South Uist on the horizon.

Park at the entrance of the long driveway at GR 691034. At the bend in the track, climb directly north up the open hillside. Visit first the east summit, for the view to Skye and Rum, then wander across to the west summit for the view north, as described above. Return by the upward route.

South Uist

Few Hebridean archipelagos can rival South Uist for scenic diversity. The island is a stunning showpiece for the best of the landscapes and nature to be found in the Western Isles: from spectacular beaches to awe-inspiring moorland wilderness, from a glorious profusion of wild flowers to the bewildering number of rare birds to be seen.

On its east side, South Uist is a rugged, barely inhabited expanse of high moorland, heather and peat bog penetrated by sea lochs, for many perhaps the quintessential Scotland. Here, a grey spine of Lewisian gneiss, the bedrock of the Outer Hebrides and half as old as the earth itself, gives rise to the highest hills in the Western Isles outside Harris and Lewis. The west side story, however, could hardly be more different: flat and fertile, with an extensive dune system and long sandy beaches. In summer, the endless acres of machair are transformed to a riot of colour, a patchwork of flower-filled meadows and cornfields, which also benefit rare ground-nesting birds such as corncrakes.

Relative to other landscape features, sand dunes move at a rapid rate. As shifting sands are washed away, blown along and redeposited, the dunes continue to reveal Neolithic, Iron Age and Viking remains, new pieces in the jigsaw of South Uist's long story of human habitation (Short Walk 15).

A paradise for budding naturalists and a hill-walker's dream, South Uist is also just perfect for the more leisurely inclined. After a day or two on South Uist, one of Scotland's remotest inhabited islands, and the stresses and strains of civilisation will seem a world away.

MAIN SETTLEMENTS

Lochboisdale, on the north shore of the sea loch of the same name, has a population of little more than 300 and is the largest township on South Uist. For visitors travelling from the south, it is the main point of arrival. Lochboisdale has a tourist information office, post office, hotel and most other essential services. It is the only settlement on the east coast, the remainder of the island's 2,000 or so population living in scattered townships along the fertile west coast plain. Kilpheder, Gerinish and Eochar are all sizeable crofting communities.

ACCESS

The Cal Mac vehicle and passenger ferry from Oban serves Lochboisdale six times a week in the summertime (no service on Sundays). Also, a private passenger-only ferry plies the Sound of Barra between Eoligarry on Barra and Ludag on South Uist, occasionally via Eriskay (telephone 01878 720238).

A British Airways Twin Otter plane serves Benbecula Airport, flights connecting with Glasgow, Barra and Stornoway. From here, South Uist is accessible by the A865 road and the causeway across the tidal sands between the two islands. There is also a causeway between Benbecula and North Uist, this effectively making all three islands one: Benbecula and the Uists. South Uist can therefore also be reached by ferry from Skye or Harris via North Uist.

ACCOMMODATION

The Lochboisdale Hotel (telephone 01878 700332) is the most convenient situation for the Oban ferry. There are one or two other hotels on the island: for outstanding views, try the Polochar Inn (telephone 01878 700215) on the south coast. A scattering of B&Bs can be found in Lochboisdale and along the west coast. For £15 per night, 289 Kilphedar is a good choice (telephone 01878 700425), a friendly B&B run by Mr and Mrs Mackinnon. For larger groups on longer stays, there are a number of self-catering options.

There is a basic SYHA hostel at Howmore (Tobha Mòr) run by the Gatliff Hebridean Hostels Trust. The hostel is a simple stone cottage sleeping eight with more bunks in recently renovated adjoining farm buildings. No advance bookings are accepted but then no one is likely to be turned away either.

PUBLIC TRANSPORT

There is a good daily bus service (W17) five or six times per day along the entire length of the A865, thus serving South Uist, Benbecula and North Uist between Lochboisdale and Lochmaddy. The Lochboisdale to South Glendale route (via Ludag pier) is served by the W29 service. Other off-the-beaten track locations are served by school buses, but obviously on schooldays only. There are no Sunday services.

Car hire is possible from Laing Motors in Lochboisdale.

ORDNANCE SURVEY LANDRANGER MAPS

Landranger sheets 22 and 31 are required to cover all of South Uist.

MAIN PLACES OF INTEREST

Beinn Mhòr (1) Walk 19
Ben Corodale (2) Walk 19
Caisteal Bheagram (3) Walk 20
Corodale Bay (4) Walk 19
Dùn Roauill (5) Walk 20

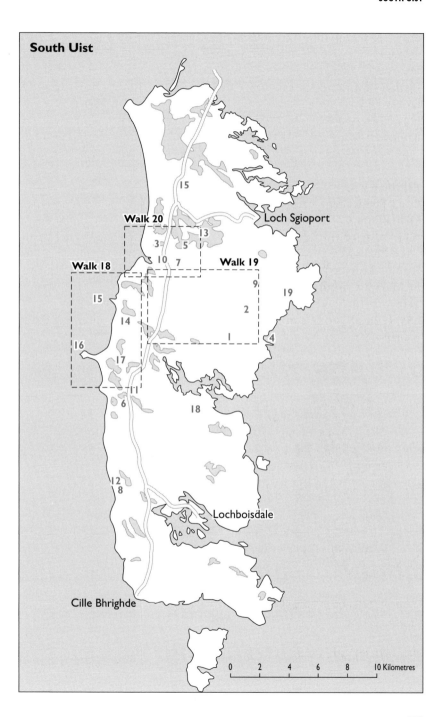

South Uist

15

Walk 20

Loch Sgioport

3
5
13

10 7

Walk 19

Walk 18

15

9

19

14

2

16

1

4

17

11

6

18

12
8

Lochboisdale

Cille Bhrighde

0   2   4   6   8   10 Kilometres

Flora MacDonald's birthplace (6) Ruins of the dwelling and a cairn commemorating the heroine, at Milton (Gearraidh Bhailteas)

Haarsal (7) Walk 20

Hallan (8) Bronze Age site; Short Walk 15

Hecla (9) Walk 19

Howmore (10) Walk 20

Kildonan Museum (11) Local history exhibitions, museum and tearoom. By A865 at Kildonan (Cill Donnain). Bronze Age and Iron Age sites on the beach.

Kilpheder (12) Viking settlement; Short Walk 15

Loch Druidibeg (13) Including NNR; Walk 20

Ormaclate Castle (14) Walk 18

'Our Lady of the Isles' (15) Statue by Sir Hugh Lorimer on the hill named Ruabhal, at GR 776408

Rubha Ardrule (**Air a' Mhuile**) (16) Headland; Walk 18

St Mary's Church (17) Walk 18

Trinival (18) Short Walk 17

Uamh Iosal (19) Souterrains and remains of wheelhouse at remote site in Glen Uisinish (Gleann Uisinis), below Hecla, at GR 843332.

Flora MacDonald's monument at Milton, South Uist

W A L K 18

Ormaclate Castle and Rubha Aird a' Mhuile Headland

Main interest and sights	Castle ruins, extensive machair, a large beach and a flat exposed headland: Ormaclate Castle (Ormacleit Castle) (14) St Mary's Church (17) Rubha Ardvule (Aird a' Mhuile) (16)
Route	Circular
Grade	Easy
Map	OS Landranger sheet 22
Starting point	Park at the roadside by Ormaclate castle, GR 741319
Finishing point	As above
Distance	9.5 km/6 mi ($3^1/_2$ hours)
Paths and terrain	Good tracks and paths traversing flat coastal area
Options	There is a continuous maze of tracks and paths running the length of the west coast machair, behind the dunes and beaches. There are therefore opportunities to extend the walk in either direction, northwards or southwards, perhaps linking with Walk 20 for a long day
Nearby walks	Walk 19, 20 and Short Walk 17
Refreshments	As for Walk 19 and at Kildonan Museum cafe, 3 km/2 mi to the south

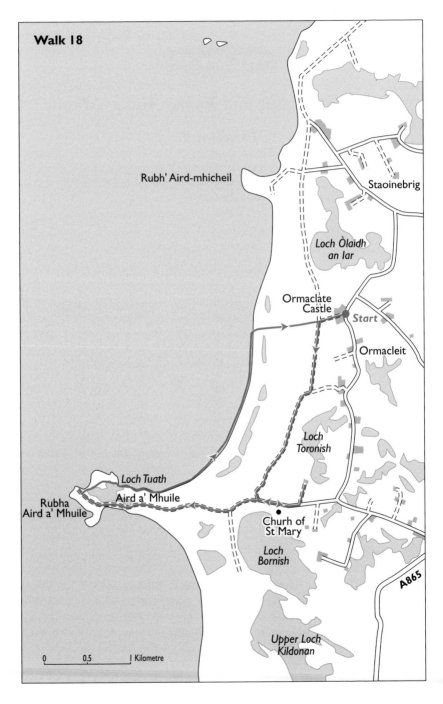

Walk 18

Rubh' Aird-mhicheil

Staoinebrig

Loch Òlaidh an Iar

Ormaclate Castle

Start

Ormacleit

Loch Toronish

Loch Tuath

Aird a' Mhuile

Rubha Aird a' Mhuile

Churh of St Mary

Loch Bornish

A865

Upper Loch Kildonan

0   0.5   I Kilometre

The vicinity of Ormacleit is a beautiful place to experience the delights of big beaches and colourful flowers. This walk also explores a ruined castle, a solitary church and a militarised headland at the westernmost point of the island.

The walk begins at **Ormaclate Castle** (14), which was completed for the Clan Ranald chief in 1708. Now only a crumbling shell remains. The Ormaclate story is a rather sad tale. The two-storey building was destroyed by a fire in 1715, some say because of a faulty kitchen chimney, others say as the result of a boisterous Jacobite party that got out of hand. On the same night as this unfortunate 'accident', the chief was killed at the Battle of Sheriffmuir. The ruins are now surrounded by croft buildings and overrun by nettles, yet some high walls and intact lintels still survive.

From the castle, follow a track westwards past some old tractors and ploughs half hidden among the cow parsley. This graveyard of farm machinery is like an outdoor museum of island crofting. Among many fascinating rusting relics are what seem to be early haymaking and harvesting machines.

At the junction of tracks, turn left. Follow another track south to where there is direct evidence of the importance of the machair to the island's crofters. There are little patches tended for potatoes, hay and a few other crops. South Uist was the first of the Hebridean islands to grow potatoes, introduced in 1743 by Clan Ranald. Crop rotation and traditional methods of crofting are here, as elsewhere, being encouraged to maintain and enhance the flora and wildlife interest. Seaweed, rather than chemicals, continues to be used as the fertiliser for the ploughed patches.

Ormaclate Castle, South Uist

When you reach Bornish, the church of **St Mary** (17) may be visited.

Otherwise, walk west from here and out on to the headland of **Rubha Ardvule** (16), named after a Viking princess called Vule. Notice that the machair is quite flat enough to be used as a football pitch, for a game that it would be impossible to play on the east side of the island. Once out on the headland itself, walk between the south shore of Loch Tuath Ardvule and the sea. The base of the circular wall of Dùn Vulan, which would have once served a defensive role, is still visible. Since the 1960s, however, the headland has been used by the Ministry of Defence as a missile range for practice in repelling invasions elsewhere. During the Falklands War, it served as firing range for Rapier missiles. There is a trig pillar at the very tip of the headland ($1^3/_4$ hours) from where the view across the sea fills a wide horizon. Looking back towards the island, the sandy beaches seem to be never-ending.

To add variation to your return, go back along the north shore of the loch, drop down to the beach and continue along the sands. When adjacent to Ormaclate Castle, simply cut across the dunes. Wherever you happen to wander on the coast there is always the chance of a wildlife surprise. White-tailed sea eagles are occasionally seen on sorties, away from their usual haunts in the mountains or at sea, looking for an easy snack of rabbit. The sight of a sea eagle unfolding its huge 3 m/10 ft-span wings at close quarters has to be one of the most spectacular sights in the world of British birds. I have seen one myself, just here at Ormacleit.

Beinn Mhòr

Main interest and sights	An ascent of South Uist's highest hill, giving rise to outstanding views: Beinn Mhòr (1) Ben Corodale (Beinn Corradail) (2) Hecla (Thacia) (9) Corodale Bay (Bàgh Chorodail) (4)
Route	Linear
Grade	Strenuous (a walk for fit and capable hill-walkers)
Map	OS Landranger sheet 22
Starting point	A865 at Abhainn Ròg, near Howmore (Tob Ha Mòr), GR 768348
Finishing point	As above
Distance	11.7 km/7¼ mi (5¼ hours)
Paths and terrain	Unpathed for most of the way but well-defined ridge approaching summit. Gradually steepening ascent over some rough terrain. Potential navigational errors
Options	There are no easier options for climbing any one of the three high hills of South Uist. Having reached the top of Beinn Mhòr, however, strong and experienced walkers might wish to then tackle Ben Corodale and Hecla to the north-northeast. Climb Ben Corodale first, via the Bealach Hellisdale. Return from Hecla by the west ridge and a long tramp across the moor. Involves nearly 1,200 m/4,000 ft of ascent (very strenuous, 8¼ hours)
Nearby walks	Walk 18 and Walk 20
Refreshments	None en route; nearest at the post office and shop on the A865 road near Howmore (1.6 km/1 mile north of starting point)

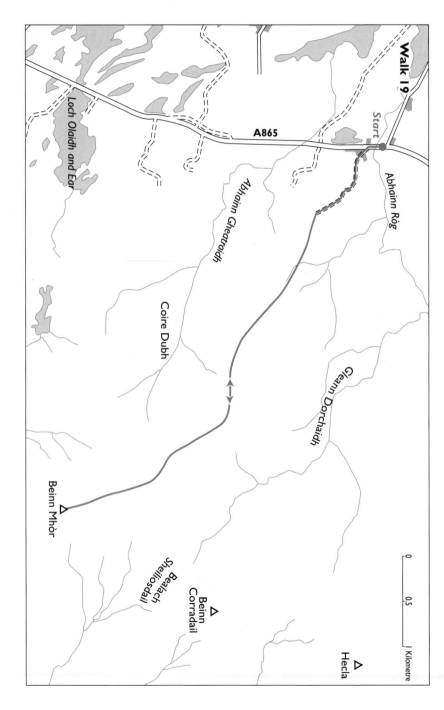

Between the two worlds of South Uist's east and west sides rises **Beinn Mhòr** (1), the island's highest hill. Located roughly centrally, its summit is the ideal place to survey barren hills and a rugged coastline on one side and a flat, fertile plain fringed by extensive shell-sand beaches on the other.

Park close to the passing place immediately north of the Abhainn Ròg. Walk south over the bridge and turn left to gain a track. Follow this to where it eventually fades away between peat cuttings. From here, strike out southeast across the unpathed moor, at first passing just north of a lochan. Then slowly climb the slopes of Maola Breac to gain the ridge rising from the Bealach Carra Dhomhnuill Ghuirm. At this point it is a good idea to look back over the ground you have just covered for reference points for regaining the track upon your return.

As you continue along the well-defined ridge, height is gained quickly and with increasing steepness. The ascent becomes more enjoyable and the views ever more spectacular.

A stone cairn that has the appearance of a hut-circle marks a summit at 608 m/1,995 ft. From this point, the ascent continues along a narrow and extremely exhilarating ridge of rock and grass. Nimble footwork and careful manoeuvring are required but there are no technical difficulties.

On the Long Isle south of Harris, Beinn Mhòr is the only hill above 610 m/2,000 ft. The main summit ($2^3/_4$ hours) has a trig pillar at 620 m/ 2,034 ft, sitting aloft a series of gneiss buttresses and cliffs that form the south wall of Coire Hellisdale (Coire Sheilesdail). The other big hills of the group, **Ben Corodale** (2) and **Hecla** (9), rise to the north of Beinn Mhòr on the other side of Glen Hellisdale (Gleann Sheilesdail). Even St Kilda, some 70 km/44 mi distant, may be seen on a very clear day. If you watch the sun rise at dawn on Easter Day from Beinn Mhòr, it is said you can see it dancing on the summit of the Skye Cuillin for joy that Christ is risen.

With human settlement having concentrated on the fertile Atlantic side, the beautiful but desolate coastline that faces the mainland has found favour with only one or two fishing communities. It was just below, however, at **Corodale Bay** (4) in 1746, that the Young Pretender discovered rocks and caves that suited his desperate need to remain elusive, the Prince's Cave being one of many such hideouts in the Isles used by the Bonnie Prince fleeing after Culloden.

Return to the main road in reverse of the upward route.

Howmore and Loch Druidibeg

Main interest and sights	Ruined medieval chapels, traditional thatch and wildlife on a National Nature Reserve: Howmore (Tobha Mòr) (10) Caisteal Bheagram (3) Loch Druidibeg (13) Dùn Roauill (Dùn Raghaill) (5) Haarsal (Thatharsal) (7)
Route	Circular
Grade	Moderate
Map	OS Landranger sheet 22
Starting point	Howmore (Tobha Mòr), GR 758363
Finishing point	As above
Distance	8.5 km/5^1/$_4$ mi (3^1/$_2$ hours)
Paths and terrain	A combination of good paths and tracks and wild and untrodden heath and grass. Straightforward ascent of a modest hill
Options	(a) Omit the climb to Haarsal by returning west to the A865 from Dùn Roauill. This is easier but no shorter (easy/moderate, 3^3/$_4$ hours) (b) Those with a particular ornithological interest will find the SNH self-guided waymarked walk around Loch Druidibeg exceptionally rewarding. Leaflets are available at the SNH Uist office at Stilligarry (Stadhlaigearraidh) (easy/moderate, 3 hours)
Nearby walks	Walk 18, Walk 19 and Short Walk 16
Refreshments	Post office shop at Howmore

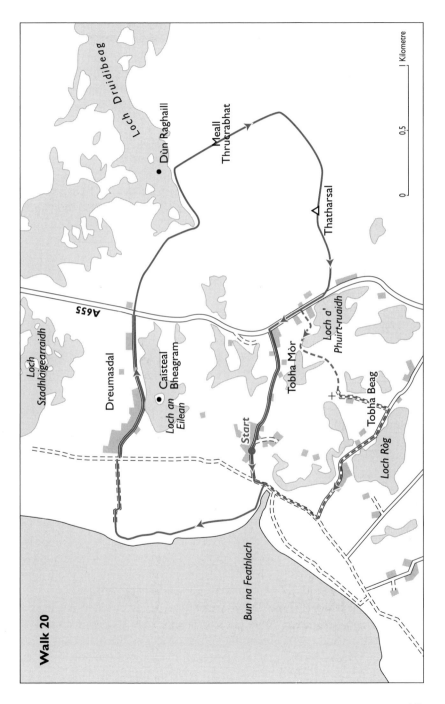

Walk 20

Loch Druidibeag

Dùn Raghaill

Meall Thrutrabhat

Thatharsal

A865

Loch Stadhlaigearraidh

Dreumasdal

Caisteal Bheagram

Loch an Eilean

Loch a' Phuirt-ruaidh

Tobha Mòr

Tobha Beag

Loch Ròg

Start

Bun na Feathlach

0   0.5   1 Kilometre

An undemanding exploration of the environs of Howmore (**Tobha Mòr**) (10), the township lying immediately southwest of Loch Druidibeg NNR, provides a perfect introduction to the island's many wonders of nature. This circular walk is not too long, yet explores the transitional area between the two contrasting landscapes, allowing you to observe the full range of wildlife and habitats typical of the Western Isles. It should involve you in no more than a morning ramble.

Begin at Howmore, where fascinating examples of traditional island black-houses come complete with rooftop mosses and grasses sprouting from coverings of thatch. Close to the Youth Hostel stand the lichen-encrusted ruins of more ancient buildings. No fewer than five churches and chapels once served this important sixteenth-century ecclesiastical complex, the largest, Teampull Mor (St Mary's Chapel), being almost 20 m (60 ft) long. A favoured burial ground for Clan Ranald chiefs, Howmore has also borne witness to many sacred sightings, not least of the Virgin Mary and even of Christ himself, who apparently raised his hand and blessed Howmore in front of a child tending her father's cows.

Walk towards the beach, then follow a track north across the machair before turning inland again from the rocks at Sgeir Dreumadail. June and July are the best times to admire the flower-scented carpets of yellow and white, of daisies, buttercups, field pansies and trefoils. Of orchids alone, 27 different species have been recorded on South Uist. Corncrakes nest in the vicinity, their presence advertised by distinctive rasping calls. Other ground-nesters include redshanks and plovers as well as those fierce defenders of territory, oystercatchers.

At Drimsdale (Dreumasdal), follow the road east, passing Loch an Eilean. The ruins of **Casteal Bheagram** (3) can be seen out in the shallow water, a late medieval tower occupying its own small island and with an underwater causeway leading out to it. It was held by the MacDonalds of Clan Ranald. Where the Drimsdale road meets the A865, go through a gate opposite and continue along a Landrover track, leading eventually to Loch Druidibeg. Then follow a stony track by the shore for about 10 minutes, walking east-northeast and arriving at a point adjacent to another scrub-covered island. The top of the crumbling walls of the best-preserved dun on South Uist, **Dùn Roauill** (5), can still be seen above the encroaching foliage.

Loch Druidibeg (13) itself is important for a variety of waterfowl, including the rare greylag geese. One obvious benefit from its designation as an NNR is woodland regeneration. The return of willow, birch and rowan and the naturalising of an old pine plantation and patches of rhododendron are transforming the ungrazed ground of the reserve into a leafy oasis.

Leave the lochside by taking to the hills immediately to the south, climbing first on to Meall Thucrabhat. From there, follow a broad, grass and heather-covered ridge that sweeps westward for just over 1 km/²/₃ mi, gently rising to 139 m/456 ft above sea level and to the trig pillar on **Haarsal** (7). This relatively isolated hill overlooks the island's two very different sides and is an exceptional viewpoint despite its modest stature. To the southeast are Beinn Mhòr and neighbouring Hecla and Ben Corodale. This trio of peaks forms the most prominent landmark on the island's mountainous spine.

By climbing Haarsal one has taken the necessary step for appreciating fully the sublime beauty of the Atlantic coastal strip: a broad emerald mantle sparkling with the waters of countless lochs, each, as many a Hebridean angler will boast, brimming with wild brown trout. And between the green mantle and the turquoise sea, an unbroken sweep of white sand extends the full 30 km/18³/₄ mi-length of the west coast. These are world-renowned beaches, yet you can have them pretty much to yourself thanks to the cooling sea breeze that blows constantly over the Western Isles. Only the very brave would swim here without a wetsuit!

Descend the west slope of Haarsal, which is quite steep but otherwise straightforward, returning to the A865 at Loch a ' Phuirt-ruaidh. Close by, in perfect timing it seems after three hours' walking, Howmore Post Office shop is there to provide necessary sustenance. Cars parked by the Youth Hostel are a further 1 km/²/₃ mi to the west, along the minor Howmore road. Alternatively, the more adventurous can make a cross-country return via a labyrinth of attractive lochans that lie between the Post Office and the Catholic church at Howbeg (Tobha Beag).

Loch Druidibeg, South Uist

Short Walks

15 HALLAN AND KILPHEDER: AN ANCIENT PAST (2 HOURS; OSLR MAP 31)

This walk is a must for those with an interest in archaeology. Fascinating remains of the Bronze Age and the Viking Age have recently been exposed in the dunes at **Hallan** (**Thallan**) (8) and **Kilpheder** (**Cille Pheadair**) (12). The erosive forces of a sea shifting steadily eastwards are partly responsible for the ongoing discoveries of South Uist's ancient past.

Park at the radio mast at GR 736217. Follow the track towards the sea and the dunes to a point west of a cemetery. A recent excavation by Cardiff University, in a sand quarry here, has uncovered the remains of a 3,000-year-old village, including an unusual double-roomed house and a large roundhouse.

Leaving the Bronze Age behind, walk south along the beach for a 2 km/1¼ mi and a 2,000 year journey forward in time. This next site is a Viking settlement in a sand cliff facing the sea. The layout of houses here suggests that they may have been forerunners of the blackhouses.

Gain the track going back northwest over the rabbit-ridden machair, not forgetting to visit the site of a wheelhouse (GR 733702 and marked as 'Aisled House' on OS map) before continuing to Hallan. Like other wheelhouses discovered in the Northern and Western Isles, this one resembles a wheel in plan: the thick outer wall forms the rim, with projecting stone piers resembling spokes, with a central fireplace at the hub. The Kilpheder wheelhouse is thought to be late Iron Age, built into the sand with probably only the roof visible above ground. Wheelhouses seem to have served a domestic purpose rather than a defensive role, despite, in some cases, having utilised the outer walls of earlier brochs and duns as ready-made rims.

16 LOCH SKIPORT (1 HOUR; OSLR MAP 22)

Loch Skiport (Sgiopoirt) is one of four sea lochs that penetrate deep into the mountainous spine of South Uist's eastern side. Exploration here is likely to fulfil all your expectations of the Scottish landscape; the surprises are revealed in the walks on the Atlantic side.

From the end of the B890 road from Loch Druidibeg (GR 828386), simply follow a track south then east, leading to shielings within about 30 minutes. The deeply indented rocky and rather forbidding coastline of Loch Skiport is a wilderness with a distinctly rugged charm. Return the same way.

17 TRINIVAL AND LOCH EYNORT (1 ¹/₂ HOURS; OSLR MAP 22)

Loch Eynort (Aineort) comes close to cutting South Uist in two, almost joining with a labyrinth of freshwater lochans on the west side. From an accessible perch on the south side of the loch, one is able to appreciate with relative ease the fjord-like coastscapes below Beinn Mhòr.

Park by the boathouse at the end of the southern fork of the road to Loch Eynort (GR 778276). Leave the road end at Unasary (Unasaraidh) by climbing the hill rising to the south, **Trinival** (Trinneabhal) (18). Ascend the unpathed but relatively dry northwest ridge direct to reach the summit at 198 m/650 ft. The views across this most mountainous region of South Uist are very impressive, as is the sight of the Minch over the flat machair and long beaches. Loch Eynort, with its countless inlets, bays and channels, is seen to wonderful effect from Trinival.

Return by the upward route or, for variation, by the ridge just to the west of the summit, also descending northwards.

A close-to-sea level alternative walk at Loch Eynort follows a path west from the end of the road on the north shore. From setting out amid trees and garden fuchsia (GR 788283), it is possible, with a little rough moorland walking, to walk right through to the open sea at Meall Mòr.

North Uist

The North Uist landscape is a glistening, lochan-studded wilderness of desolate beauty or a sunken water-sodden quagmire of desperate monotony: exactly which depends on your disposition and, as always, the weather. Beyond doubt is one's sense of being on another world.

North Uist is a deep peatland with a mosaic of intricately entangled lochans, a landscape as much of water as of land. It is far flatter than the other Uist to the south yet broadly conforms to the general character of the Long Isle, with magnificent expanses of sand and machair along its west coast. Of particular historical note is that at least half of all the Neolithic chambered cairns in the Western Isles are to be found in North Uist, including the best preserved of them all, Barpa Langass (Short Walk 18).

The machair at **Balranald National Nature Reserve** (2) supports some of the highest densities in the world of certain species of nesting wading birds, in particular dunlin, ringed plover, lapwing, redshank and oystercatcher. The reserve was established in 1966, primarily to preserve the breeding habitat of the rare red-necked phalarope, but it is also important for the corncrake. On the east side, Loch Maddy (Loch nam Madadh) supports a unique combination of intertidal plants and animals noted for their tolerance to changes in salinity. Because of a complex network of lagoons, inlets and rapids, here salt and fresh waters become intermixed.

Sadly, many of North Uist's ground-nesting birds are currently threatened by an invasion of mink, voracious predators of ground-nesting birds. A northern offensive from Harris, where minks have long been established, has already begun. Strong swimmers, mink have begun to breach the Sound of Harris and are now proving difficult to eradicate because they are so completely at home feeding and hiding in the numerous indentations of the North Uist coastline. The maze of inlets, lochs and interconnecting burns is the perfect highway along which mink can travel. At the same time, such terrain makes them difficult to trap. As it is, North Uist remains essentially a bird-watcher's paradise and the perfect place for all those with webbed feet.

MAIN SETTLEMENTS

Lochmaddy, an attractive township, is the principal administrative centre and ferry terminal for North Uist. There are shops, a hotel, a post office, court houses, an outdoor centre and most services, including a tourist information office. Lochmaddy was one of the finest harbours in eighteenth-century Scotland (see Options, Walk 21). Crofting and fishing communities are strung out along the A865, mostly on the north and west coasts, the largest being Bayhead (Ceann a' Bháigh).

ACCESS
Lochmaddy is the main ferry terminal for Cal Mac vehicle and passenger ferries from Uig on Skye, operating daily including Sundays. If travelling from the south by road, the usual route is to first cross by car ferry from Oban to Lochboisdale on South Uist. From the north there is a daily car ferry service from late March to late October (except Sundays) between Leverburgh on Harris and Otternish, at the north end of North Uist. To travel by air, fly to Benbecula, which is connected to North Uist by the A865 across a causeway.

ACCOMMODATION
The Lochmaddy Hotel (telephone 01876 500331) is close to the ferry pier, with Langass Lodge (telephone 01816 580285) at Loch Euphoirt, near Barpa Langass Chambered Cairn, the more secluded option. There is plenty of B&B accommodation available and even more cottages available for rent.

The most comfortable hostel accommodation is at the newly renovated croft house overlooking the tidal sands at Carnach, 'Taigh Mo Sheanair' (telephone 01876 58246). An SYHA hostel in Lochmaddy is run by the Gatliff Hebridean Hostels Trust and sleeps 36, but only between May and September.

PUBLIC TRANSPORT
The W17 bus service, which also serves South Uist and Benbecula, operates five to six times a day between the causeway in the south to Otternish in the north, via Lochmaddy and the east side of North Uist. The A865, which skirts the north and west coasts, is served about three times daily by the W18 service between Lochmaddy and Clachan. Postbuses operate between Lochmaddy and Benbecula Airport once a day. Other postbuses serve Baleshare from Lochmaddy via Langass and Clachan as well as Benbecula Airport from Tigharry by the west coast. No buses of any kind operate on a Sunday.

ORDNANCE SURVEY LANDRANGER MAPS
Landranger sheets 18 and 22 are required to cover all of North Uist.

MAIN PLACES OF INTEREST
Baleshare (1) Island off the west coast with extensive machair and beaches; thriving crofting population; access via causeway or across sands at low tide.
Balranald NNR (2) See Introduction, page 150

Barpa Langass Chambered Cairn (3) Short Walk 18

Bhorogaigh (4) Tiny uninhabited island on North Uist's Cockle Strand

Clettraval Chambered Cairn (5) Of 'Clyde' type and unique in the Western Isles; also remains of Iron Age wheelhouse, GR 749713

Dùn an Sticer (6) Broch on island in loch near Newtonferry (Port nan Long), accessible via stone causeway, GR 897777

Eaval (7) Highest hill in North Uist, in southeast corner

Lochmaddy (8) see Main Settlements, page 150, and Walk 21

Lochmaddy Museum and Arts Centre (**Tàigh Chearsabhagh**) (9) Local history and children's activities in Lochmaddy (telephone 01876 500293, closed January and February)

Marrival (10) Superb hilltop viewpoint to Loch Scadaway

Na Fir Bhreige (11) Three standing stones on northwest flank of Blashaval

North Lee (12) Walk 21

Pobull Fhinn Stone Circle (13) Short Walk 18

Scolpaig Arches (14) Short Walk 19

Scolpaig Tower (15) Only 'folly' in the Western Isles, built in nineteenth century on remains of dun in Loch Scolpaig, GR 731750

South Lee (16) Walk 21

St Peter's Cross (17) 1 km/²/₃ mi southwest of Scolpaig, GR 726744

Trinity Temple (**Teampull na Trionaid**) (18) Important archaeological and ecclesiastical site. One of the largest pre-Reformation churches in the Western Isles and a major centre of learning in medieval times, GR 816603

Uist Animal Visitor Centre (19) At Bayhead (Ceann a' Bháigh) (telephone 01876 510223)

Uist Outdoor Centre (20) At Lochmaddy for diving, water sports, climbing, etc. (telephone 01876 500480)

Unival Chambered Cairn (21) Neolithic, on south flank of Unival (Uineabhal); remains of Iron Age house at same site, GR 800668

Stone Age tomb on barren Unival

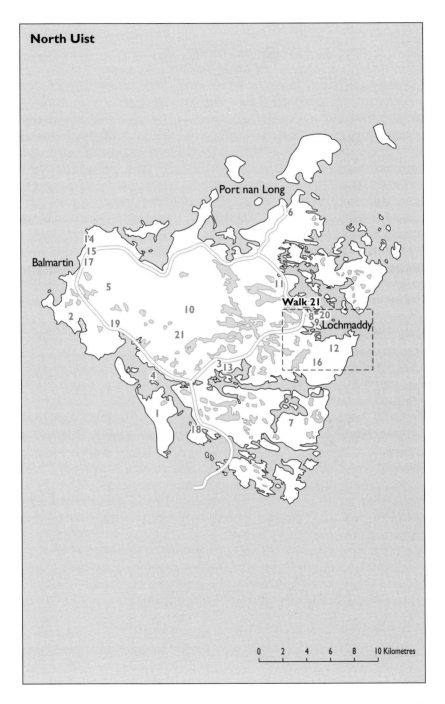

North Uist

Port nan Long

Balmartin

14
15
17
5
2
19
10
21
3 13
4
1
18
7

6

11

Walk 21
8 20
9 Lochmaddy
12
16

0   2   4   6   8   10 Kilometres

North Lee and South Lee

Main interest and sights	Views across an unusual chequerboard of land and water: Lochmaddy (8) North Lee (Li a' Tuath) (12) South Lee (Li a' Deas) (16)
Route	Circular
Grade	Moderate/strenuous
Map	OS Landranger sheet 18
Starting point	Small parking bay on A867 by Loch na Maighdein, GR 895679
Finishing point	As above
Distance	10.2 km/6^1/$_4$ mi (5 hours)
Paths and terrain	Pathless for the approach, traversing peaty and wet terrain. The hills are rough and steep in places but are of modest height and not difficult. Ability to navigate with a map and compass is essential
Options	A walk around Lochmaddy. From the main pier walk to the Post Office then turn right past New Court House, over the footbridge to Sponish House and back by a track to the main road ('Western Isles Walks' leaflet, available from the Tourist Information centre in Lochmaddy)
Nearby walks	Short Walk 18
Refreshments	Lochmaddy Hotel and shops in Lochmaddy

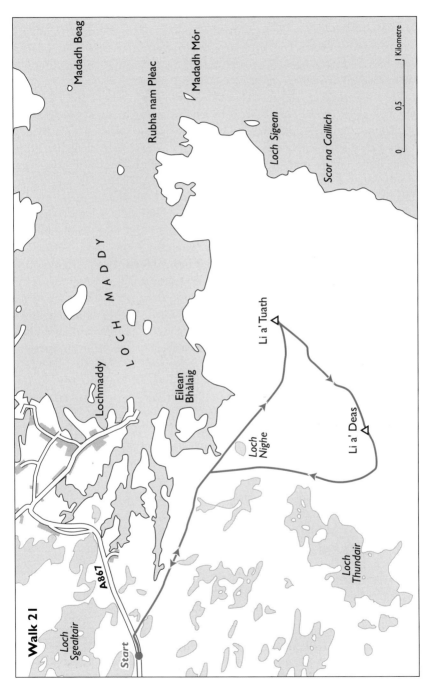

Walk 21

Loch Sgealtair

A867

Start

Lochmaddy

LOCH MADDY

Madadh Beag

Rubha nam Plèac

Madadh Mór

Loch Sigean

Scor na Caillich

Eilean Bhalaig

Li a' Tuath

Loch Nighe

Li a' Deas

Loch Thundair

1 Kilometre

0.5

0

It is on the twin protrusions of gneiss rock that rise highest above the shores of Loch Maddy that one finds the most perfect of viewpoints for admiring the remarkable North Uist landscape, an unfathomable tangle of peat banks, low hills, lochs and burns. The approach to these two hills on foot from the main road offers walkers a taste of something unique.

From the parking bay, walk west along the road for about 200 m and go through a gate on the right. Walk between the two lochans and proceed east-southeast to another gate, close to one of the many inlets of Loch Maddy. One such inlet, possibly this very one, is said to have once sheltered a unicorn. But despite witnesses' accounts of 'a tall awkward beast with long legs', it was suggested that the creature was in fact a narwhal. Here, the sea reaches inland, seeking to make contact with the shores of freshwater lochs.

Continue over rough and peaty terrain, aiming for the northernmost of the summits ahead of you. Beyond a third gate, trend a little more to the south to reach a fourth gate close to Loch Nighe. Southeast of this point, the gradient rises gently up to a fifth gate, on the hillside below **North Lee** (12). From here, ascend a steep grassy slope east to gain the trig pillar at 250 m/820 ft (2 hours).

From this lower one of North Lee's summits there is a fine view across the sheltered waters and numerous islands of Loch Maddy. Guarding Loch Maddy's entrance are two rock masses known as the 'Maddies', Madadh Beag and Madadh Mór, from which the loch takes its name. Some say they resemble watchdogs and that this is also their purpose. A third 'dog', Madadh Gruamach, lies a bit farther south. The buildings of **Lochmaddy** (8) (see Options) are clustered behind the pier. If your timing is right, it is fascinating to watch the approaching Cal Mac ferry from Skye negotiate the obstacle-ridden waters of the loch. It must have been a much busier scene, however, in the seventeenth century, when the loch harboured as many as 400 fishing vessels. The view west across the interior of North Uist is of lochs and lochans as far as the eye can see.

The main summit of North Lee and that of **South Lee** (16) (3 hours) are both reached by continuing southwest. There is a tiny lochan in the *bealach* between the two from where a steep zigzagging path leads up to the top of South Lee, the higher hill (the two summits of which are less than 10 minutes apart). Eaval is the prominent hill to the south, North Uist's highest, and one that requires to be approached by boat.

Descend west, then bearing north from between the two summits of South Lee to reach a gate at the bottom (GR 913656). From Guala Mhór head north across open country and aim for a point between Loch na Hostrach and Loch Nighe. You will then regain familiar ground, that over which you began your endeavour, which provides the best means of finding the road again.

Short Walks

18 BARPA LANGASS (1¹/₄ HOURS; OSLR 18)

Of the island's nineteen or so chambered cairns, **Barpa Langass** (3) is the most impressive. This walk also visits the finest stone circle in North Uist. Park at the end of the little road to Langass Lodge Hotel (GR 838652). Walk towards Loch Langass, but before reaching the shore take the path off to the left leading to **Pobull Fhinn Stone Circle** (13). It is sited on the south flank of Ben Langass (Beinn Langais), overlooking the loch. Only about half of the 48 stones are still standing and most of these are tilted to an angle, but the irregular oval arrangement of the circle is still apparent. It was constructed about 2000 BC although, as with stone circles elsewhere, its original purpose is a matter for conjecture.

Continue to the summit of Ben Langass from where there is a fine view over many lochs. Barpa Langass Chambered Cairn is about 700 m/¹/₂ mi beyond, lower down on the northwest side of the hill, close to the A867 and rises prominently some 4.2 m/14 ft above the moorland. The cairn almost certainly predates the stone circle; with care, the burial chamber can still be entered from the east side. Follow marker posts back to the hotel road.

19 SCOLPAIG ROCK ARCHES (1¹/₄ HOURS; OSLR 18)

Two rock arches on Griminish Point (Rubha Ghriminis), at the northwest corner of North Uist, constitute the island's most impressive natural features. When severe weather stirs the sea, they are a spectacular sight.

Park on the grass at the end of the track at Scolpaig (GR 730753) and simply follow the coastline north below Beinn Scolpaig. On reaching Griminish Point (under ¹/₂ hour), you will see the arches on the near side of the headland. The inner entrances of both can be viewed by descending carefully into the blowhole between them. Their sea-facing sides are best seen from the coastal cliffs on either side. During gales, such is the force of water through the arches that the resulting waterspout can be seen from ten miles away at sea.

Return the same way.

Harris

Harris and Lewis are really one island, one that constitutes the largest landmass of the Outer Hebrides and the true Long Isle of old (before Benbecula, the Uists and Barra were added). They are more generally regarded as two separate islands, however, North Harris's formidable mountains being both an effective geographical as well as social barrier. Variations in respective spoken dialects of Gaelic are recognised on both sides of the upland divide. The two communities have separate histories, identities and landscapes. Harris is rugged with extensive sands whereas, for the most part, Lewis is a vast low-lying peat bog with a multiplicity of small lochans. One must look to a common faith between the communities to find something that they share. At this northern end of the Long Isle, the Free Presbyterian Church of Scotland is dominant although it has, as in the Highlands, welcomed and encouraged Gaelic language and culture (unlike the earlier Protestant church of John Knox, which tried to suppress it). In salmon farming, tourism, crofting and tweed cloth, they also share similar economies.

Harris itself if divided into two parts at the point where **West Loch Tarbert** (26) and East Loch Tarbert almost join, constricting the land to a thread barely half a kilometre/third of a mile across at high tide. North Harris is the most mountainous part of the Long Isle with the highest peaks. First impressions are of an imposing and inhospitable wilderness, yet it possesses many fascinating aspects that are easily accessible to the curious and the adventurous. The Forest of Harris is an important deer forest and ideal eagle territory; it is said that golden eagles nest here at a higher density than almost anywhere else in Europe.

South Harris is a greener place, especially on the west side where the machair is extensive. Although not as clearly demarcated, South Harris has much of the landscape character of the Uists, rugged and heavily indented along its eastern coast with fantastic beaches, among the finest in the Hebrides, on the west coast.

The east coast of South Harris is puckered with numerous tiny inlets and sea lochs. This is known as the **Bays District** (1), where a succession of sheltered natural harbours find favour with small fishing communities. The fertile machair on the west side is exploited for the growing of wind-resistant crops and for grazing cattle. Apart from the obvious lure of its empty beaches, the church at Rodel is the 'jewel in the crown' of Harris's tourist attractions.

MAIN SETTLEMENTS

Tarbert is the largest settlement on Harris, where all essential services are located, including a tourist information office. Most of the town's buildings and the ferry pier are at the head of East Loch Tarbert. The only other settlements of any size are on South Harris, at Northton (Tàobh Tuath) and at Leverburgh (An t-Ob) as well as the scattering of tiny fishing hamlets in the Bays District, Drinishader and Geocrab having post office stores.

ACCESS

The Cal Mac vehicle and passenger ferry from Uig (Skye) calls at Tarbert six days a week, twice a day in summer, less often in winter. A car ferry also operates in the Sound of Harris three or four times a day, providing a service between Otternish (North Uist) and Leverburgh (South Harris). There is no service on either route on a Sunday.

Stornoway (Lewis), from which there is a ferry service to Ullapool, is one hour's drive from Tarbert. Regular British Airways flights serve Stornoway direct from Glasgow and Inverness. From Glasgow flights also operate via Barra and Benbecula.

ACCOMMODATION

A wide choice of hotel, B&B and self-catering accommodation can be found, mostly on South Harris. Tarbert is the most convenient base if you want to explore the mountains, where the Harris Hotel (telephone 01859 502154) is a year-round possibility. The more scenic options, however, are in the Bays or at Northton.

There are four hostel/bunkhouses on Harris. The two SYHA hostels are at Stocinis in the Bays and at Rheinigeadal, west of Tarbert. For other budget options, the independent hostel at Drinishader (telephone 01859 511255) can be highly recommended for its superb coastal situation alone. There is also the Rockview Bunkhouse in Tarbert (telephone 01859 502211).

PUBLIC TRANSPORT

The W13 (east side) and W10 (west side) bus services operate in South Harris, both about four times per day. The W10 route continues through on the A859 to Stornoway. The W12 serves Hushnish, the W15 Scalpay and the less frequent W11 Rhenigidale on North Harris. All services operate through or from Tarbert although there are no buses on Sundays.

ORDNANCE SURVEY LANDRANGER MAPS

Landranger sheets 13, 14 and 18 are required to cover all of Harris. Sheet 14 is all you need for the 'Bays' and the main mountains of North Harris.

MAIN PLACES OF INTEREST

The Bays (1) Walk 22

Barvemor Studios (2) Gallery and café at Scaristavore (Sgarasta Mhor)

Bealach Eòrabhat (3) Walk 22

Chaipaval (Ceapabhal) (4) 339 m/1,065 ft summit of the Toe Head peninsula from which there are sweeping views. Short Walk 20

Clett Ard (5) Short Walk 22

Clisham (6) Highest summit in the Western Isles; in the Forest of North Harris

Co Leis Thu (7) In Northton, genealogical research and family history resource centre. Exhibitions open to the public

Gleann Chliostair (8) Walk 23

Glen Scaladale (9) Glen from which rises the 'horseshoe' of Harris's highest peaks

Glen Ulladale (10) Walk 23

Golden Road, The (11) Walk 22

Loch Seaforth (12) 30 km/18 mi fjord-like channel of sea water that straddles the boundary between Harris and Lewis. Short Walk 22

Loch Ulladale (13) Walk 23

Luskentyre Sands (14) Walk 22

MacLeod's Stone (Clach Mhic Leòid) (15) Short Walk 21

Northton Bay (16) Joins with Scarasta Sands to form a beautiful and extensive machair-backed beach in South Harris. Short Walk 20

Scalpay (Scalpaigh) (17) Small but scenic island reached by car ferry from Kyles in a few minutes

Scalpay Community Centre (18) Sports hall, pool and café on the island

Scarasta Sands (19) See Northton Bay

South Harris Historical Society (20) Based at Leverburgh (An t-Ob); social and natural history exhibits

Sròn Ulladale (21) Walk 23

St Clement's Church, Rodel (22) Outstanding medieval church, unique in its rectangular design, at southern tip of Harris. Built in 1500 by Alastair Crotach, the eighth MacLeod of Dunvegan; his tomb is in the church

Tarbert Local History Society (23) In the Old School Hostel

Teampall na h-Uidhe (24) Short Walk 20

Toe Head (25) Short Walk 20

West Loch Tarbert (26) Large sea loch that separates South Harris from North Harris

Whaling Station (27) Remains of old whaling station, operational until 1929. Located at Bunavoneadar

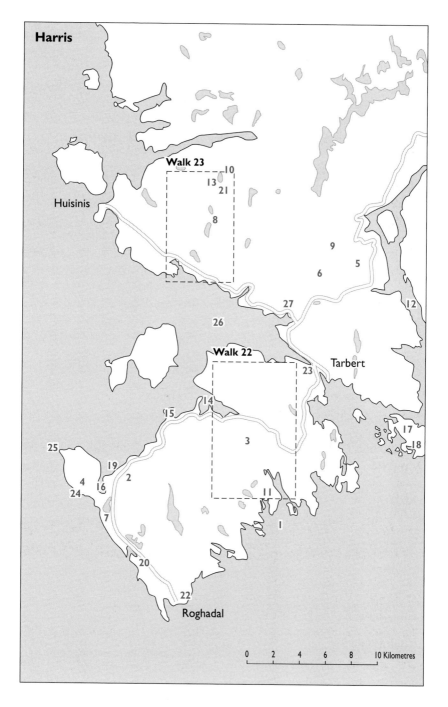

Harris

Huisinis

Walk 23

10

13
21

8

9

6
5

27

12

26

Walk 22

23

Tarbert

14

15

17

3
18

25

19

4
2

16

24

7

11

1

20

22

Roghadal

0   2   4   6   8   10 Kilometres

South Harris:
Coast to Coast via the Bealach Eòrobhat

Main interest and sights	Coast-to-coast exploration of a diversity of contrasting landscapes and wildlife habitats: The Bays (Na Baigh) (1) The Golden Road (11) Bealach Eòrabhat (3) Luskentyre Sands (Tràigh Losgaintir) (14)
Route	Circular
Grade	Moderate
Map	OS Landranger sheet 14
Starting point	Road junction at Loch Stockinsh, GR 127930
Finishing point	As above (or Luskentyre Sands)
Distance	14 km/8³/₄ mi (4¹/₂ hours)
Paths and terrain	Rough, often wet, moorland path through Bealach Eòrabhat. Easy return. No steep or sustained gradients
Options	(a) Linear route – return from Luskentyre Sands back over the *bealach* if you wish to avoid tarmac and traffic (moderate, 4¹/₂ hours) (b) Through route – if you can arrange transport back from Luskentyre Sands (easy/moderate, 2¹/₄ hours)
Nearby walks	Short Walk 21
Refreshments	None en route. Nearest at Tarbert for shops, bars and cafés

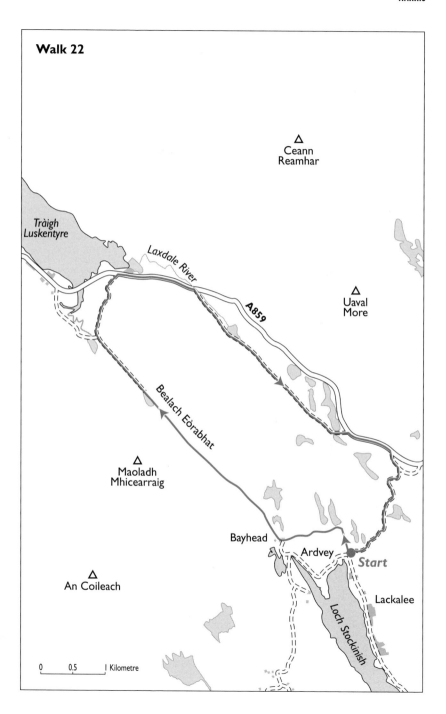

Walk 22

Ceann
Reamhar

Tràigh
Luskentyre

Laxdale River

A859

Uaval
More

Bealach Eòrabhat

Maoladh
Mhicearraig

Bayhead

Ardvey

Start

An Coileach

Lackalee

Loch Stockinish

0   0.5   1 Kilometre

The joy of this walk is the experience of transition. It follows a coast-to-coast path that was once used by funeral parties in search of a site that did not require the breaking of solid rock to bury their dead. It links the Little Minch with the Atlantic, two very different seas and two contrasting coastlines. Walking from east to west one experiences landscape changes and a corresponding shift in wildlife habitats, from hard rock to machair, from acidic to alkaline. Before reaching the finest tongue of sand on Harris, you will see freshwater lochs on the wild moor. The flora and fauna are as rich and varied as the terrain is diverse. The area has been designated a Site of Special Scientific Interest.

The walk begins at Loch Stockinish, one of the longer of the **Bays** (1), on the extremely rugged coastline extending south of Tarbert. This is an area of very old, very hard rock, yielding at most a sparse covering of acidic peat and only sporadic patches of fertile ground. Indeed, so difficult is the terrain that the tortuous strip of tarmac that joins the little fishing villages, built in the 1930s, was completed only at great expense the road thus becoming known as **The Golden Road** (11).

Start off on the path going north, signposted 'To Luskentyre (west side)'. After five minutes, at the first loch, turn left and at Bayhead go over the footbridge. Follow the west bank of a burn upstream on a path highlighted by marker posts. This east side of the pass is a landscape of grey Lewisian gneiss outcrops, the vegetation sparse and typically of the upland heath type. The path is clear, although frequently waterlogged, rising over rough terrain while becoming increasingly confined between the heights of West Stocklett and the crags of Maoladh Mhicearraig.

The top of the pass is a place to rest, as was once the habit of the funeral corteges travelling from the Bays to Seilebost, to where there was enough soil to bury the dead. At the **Bealach Eòrabhat** (3) a very different coastscape emerges: pale sands and turquoise seas.

A straightforward descent from the top of the Bealach continues past salt marsh and machair and finally reaches tidal flats and sand dunes. There are new flowers to look for, different birds on the wing and many shades of colour. **Luskentyre Sands** (14) are the place to see wading birds, including greenshank and oystercatcher, and ducks such as scooter and eider duck. The vast and empty sands of Luskentyre are also a place of legend. They were once made up of grains of pure gold, and all who wished could take what they needed. That is until a greedy man came with pony and panniers and carried off all he could with the intention of selling it on the mainland. He went on his way with his load so heavy that, when a storm blew up, he, his boat and his precious cargo all sank. Thus the beach turned from gold to ordinary sand, but once a year it does still turn back to gold again as the sun is setting over the sea, when it gleams for a moment till no one can behold it undazzled. Thus we are reminded of the lesson.

The right-hand fork of the track from Loch Carran leads down to the A859 at the head of the bay. Follow the main road southeast, through the valley of the Laxdale River, using the track that was once the old road to Tarbert. This avoids the traffic and the tarmac for a 3 km/2 mi stretch before reaching the Golden Road (first left) and thus completing the circuit.

W A L K 23

North Harris: Glen Ulladale

Main interest and sights	The massive overhang of rock that dominates the mountain wilderness of Glen Ulladale: Gleann Chliostair (8) Glen Ulladale (10) Sròn Ulladale (21) Loch Ulladale (13)
Route	Linear
Grade	Moderate
Map	OS Landranger sheets 13 or 14
Starting point	At beginning of track by the outflow to Lochan Beag on the A887, GR 053078
Finishing point	As above
Distance	14.5 km/9 mi ($4^3/_4$ hours)
Paths and terrain	Good track south of Loch Chliostair Dam and excellent stalkers' path thereafter. The only significant gradient is a sharp 150 m/490 ft descent and re-ascent to/from Glen Ulladale. Wet ground close to Loch Ulladale
Options	From Loch Ulladale, return by skirting around the north side of Sròn Ulladale. Continue south up into the broad corrie, bearing right on to Muladal. Descend to Loch Ashavat on the west side (moderate/strenuous, $5^3/_4$ hours; allow an extra $^3/_4$ hour to also gain the summit of Sròn Ulladale, an excellent viewpoint)
Nearby walks	None; nearest is Walk 22
Refreshments	None en route; nearest at Tarbert for shops, bars and cafés

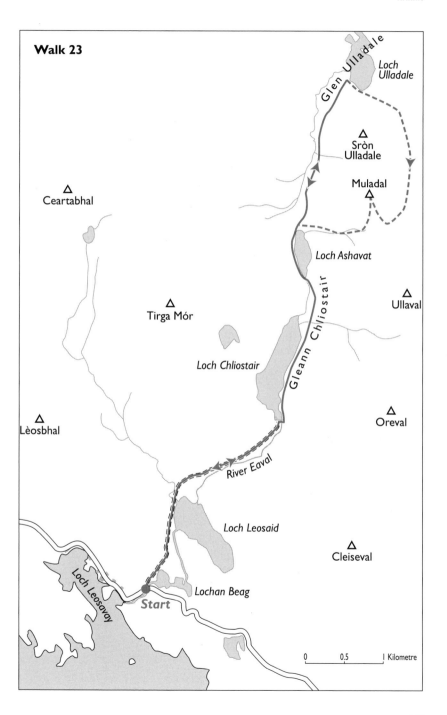

Walk 23

Glen Ulladale

Loch
Ulladale

Sròn
Ulladale

Muladal

Ceartabhal

Loch Ashavat

Ullaval

Tirga Mór

Gleann Chliostair

Loch Chliostair

Lèosbhal

Oreval

River Eaval

Loch Leosaid

Cleiseval

Loch Leosavay

Start

Lochan Beag

0   0.5   1 Kilometre

The topographical highlight of the west side of the beautiful but very desolate Forest of Harris is not a high mountain but a massive overhanging cliff. All those who venture to it, from rock climbers to geologists, return of the opinion that **Sròn Ulladale** (21) is one of the finest rock features in the Hebrides. This massive grey bulge of Lewisian gneiss inhabits the untamed domain of the red deer and overlooks remote lochs and streams brimming with trout and salmon. Consequently, and by good fortune, an excellent track and stalkers' path allow walkers to penetrate this wilderness without difficulty. Beginning by the coast of West Loch Tarbert and terminating within a whisker of Lewis, this walk almost completely traverses the Forest of Harris from south to north.

A broken tarmac track, used by a hydroelectric scheme's vehicles, allows for an easy start for 3 km/1³/₄ mi to the dam at Loch Chliostair. From the dam, gain the stalkers' path heading north into **Gleann Chliostair** (8) at first beside the east shore of Loch Chliostair followed by a walk along the west shore of Loch Ashavat. Here, in its upper reaches, the glen becomes confined and hemmed in by steep mountain slopes on either side.

From the north end of Loch Ashaval one is rewarded by a first view across the watery recesses of **Glen Ulladale** (10). High cliffs demarcate both sides of the glen, but undoubtedly the most arresting sight is the west face of Sròn Ulladale, a wall of cliffs, breathtaking in their stature. A sharp descent on a now less defined path into Glen Ulladale soon brings you directly below the south buttress. This magnificent wall of ancient grey rock, 250 m/820 ft high for over a kilometre, terminates at the 'nose' at the north end.

From the fishing hut at the shore of dark and peaty **Loch Ulladale** (13) (2¹/₂ hours), take time to contemplate the vast shadow cast across the water by Sròn Ulladale. This bulging nose of rock, an overhang towering 270 m/ 886 ft above, assumes the presence of some Herculean sentinel but one that fails to fend off a growing number of dedicated gravity-defying rock climbers, its impossible profile seeming only to heighten the challenge.

Loch Ulladale occupies a remote setting, where, apart from climbers, one's only other likely contact with the human race may be the lure-casting occupant of a rowing boat out on the water. Otherwise all is peaceful and still, only the ripples from a surfacing trout or the distant call of a red-throated diver breaking the silence.

The way back is in reverse of the outward route, unless you feel the pull of Sròn Ulladale drawing you to its summit (see Options).

Short Walks

SOUTH HARRIS

20 TEAMPALL NA H-UIDHE (1³/₄ HOURS; OSLR MAP 18)

This walk visits the ruins of a late medieval chapel and explores some of the most beautiful coastal scenery on Harris. There is much of interest for enthusiasts of both the human and natural history of the Hebrides. Hill-walkers might wish to climb **Chaipaval** (4).

Beginning at **Northton** (Tuobh Tuath) (16), walk north across the machair and follow the path behind the sandy bays along the coast on the west side. The diversity of the flora is extremely rich, including many different orchids such as the northern marsh orchid. Ragged robin and yellow flag are common in the wetter areas. Note the rust marks on the iron-rich rocks by the shore, possibly why **Toe Head** (25) was favoured by Iron Age settlers. The layout of grassy mounds and a profusion of nettles are the telltale signs of a more recent settlement, a pre-clearance township.

Gneiss outcrops on the beach below Rubh' an Teampaill exhibit red feldspar banding, a mineral quarried here during the Second World War for electrical insulation. The chapel of **Teampall na h-Uidhe** (24) occupies its own tiny headland. Built in 1537 on the site of an Iron Age fort and occupying an excellent lookout to the western approaches, only a shell now remains. However, some of the existing stonework is very fine.

For better views across the magnificent sands sweeping towards **Scarasta** (19), return by the track to the east.

21 MACLEOD'S STONE (CLACH MHIC LEÒID) (UP TO 1 HOUR; OSLR MAP 18)

MacLeod's Stone (15) is the best example of a standing stone on Harris. Park at the parking bay by the A859 (GR 037963) and follow the waymarked route across Tràigh Iar sands. For a better view of the surrounding coast, climb to the top of the headland at 61 m/200 ft. Return the same way.

NORTH HARRIS

22 CLETT ARD (2 HOURS; OSLR MAP 13 OR 14)

Clett Ard (5) is a hill of modest height and is easy to climb. From its summit there are fine views across **Loch Seaforth** (12), a 23 km/14 mi fjord-like channel of sea water that straddles the boundary between Harris and Lewis, its shores riven with lazy-beds. Part of a great deer estate, on the edge of a forbidding upland domain from which Clisham rises above all, Clett Ard gives a preview of what to expect of the highest hills on Harris.

Begin at GR 183098, at the bridge over the Scaladale River. Walk south along the road for 400 m/¼ mi to gain the path below Caisteal Ard and then strike off to the left up over the firmer ground of Clett Ard's northwest ridge. From the summit, come down on the west side and descend the path north and back to the A859.

Loch Seaforth

Lewis

Lacking the obvious scenic splendour of Harris, Lewis however is extremely rich in historic and prehistoric sites. Monuments of human habitation stretch back some five or six millennia. At **Callanish** (5) stand the most important and impressive Neolithic ceremonial stones and circles in Scotland. At **Dun Carloway** (7) is the best-preserved Iron Age antiquity in the Hebrides, and a famous find on a west coast beach tells us that between energetic bouts of raping, pillaging and bloodletting, the Norsemen found time for a game of chess. During the past decade, a number of traditional Lewis dwellings, blackhouses, have been restored, providing an insight into life on the island over the last few hundred years.

Lewis has a long history of suffering: some would say a woeful saga of bad luck and misfortune. The island has endured a succession of Norse raids, repression under both the Scottish and English crowns and, like other low, wet islands, countless famines, fevers and epidemics. Hebrideans who have stayed healthy and lived to a great age have been, typically, those of mountainous islands. Lewis lacks extensive areas of machair, so good arable and grazing land has always been in short supply. For Lewis, the description 'wet desert' seems particularly apt. But much of Lewis is prosperous now, with more than a third of the population in thriving **Stornoway** (25), by far the largest town in the Hebrides.

Lewis has hills, most notably at Uig and at Park (Pairc), but these are neither as grand nor of the stature of those on North Harris. The island gives its name to Lewisian gneiss, one of the world's oldest rocks, shaped into the above-mentioned hills and, in fact, constituting much of the landscape of northwest Scotland. Such a geology results in low-nutrient topsoil, supporting little more than heather-clad peat bogs. On Lewis, the bleak moorland is peppered with the glistening waters of dozens of lochans and scattered with the remains of shieling huts. Peat cutting remains a widespread practice. Dark blocks of this most traditional of fuels, left drying in huge piles on top of black quarried banks, is a common sight on Lewis. The shieling life, however, has disappeared forever, the days when the simple stone and turf shelters of the open moor and hill were used in summer by cattle grazers.

As elsewhere in the Hebrides, fishing and crofting have always been central to the island economy. Stornoway was once a major fishing port, and whaling was important in Lewis until the early twentieth century. Lewis is also the main centre for the production of the thread used for Harris Tweed, still woven on hand looms and very much a cottage industry. Guided tours at one or two Harris Tweed mills on the island are an option for a wet day. Plans are well advanced for a £500 million wind farm on Lewis, set to be the world's largest onshore wind farm and one that will perhaps act as catalyst in attracting further wave and tidal power stations.

Lewis possesses a few notable pale sandy beaches where rugged cliffs give way to wide open bays. Above all, Lewis is a land of big skies and long low horizons.

MAIN SETTLEMENTS

Travelling through the Long Isle from the south, bustling Stornoway, with its supermarkets, restaurants, banks, Victorian villas and, most strikingly of all, trees, comes as a bit of a shock. A long-established burgh town with 8,000 inhabitants, there is nothing else quite like it in the Western Isles. Everything you could want is here, and it has the only tourist information office in the Outer Hebrides that is open all year.

Lewis has a population of over 20,000, with other large settlements at Port of Ness, Barvas, Callanish, Knock, Back and Balallan.

ACCESS

Stornoway is served by Cal Mac MV *Isle of Lewis*, the largest car ferry operating on the west coast of Scotland, which sails from Ullapool two or three times daily. The car ferry service to Tarbet (Harris) from Uig (Skye) may be the faster crossing for visiting Lewis when travelling up from more southern parts of the mainland.

Stornoway has an airport, with British Airways flights direct from Glasgow and Inverness as well as via Barra and Benbecula.

ACCOMMODATION

The accommodation options for Lewis are numerous, with hotels, B&Bs and self-catering cottages possibly even outnumbering those on Skye. Perhaps because of the competition, very good value-for-money B&Bs can be found in Stornoway. Try Fernlea at 9 Matheson Road (telephone 01851 702125).

There are five hostels on Lewis although just one in Stornoway, the Stornoway Backpackers Hostel (telephone 01851 703628). Other independent hostels are at Galson Farm and at Laxdale. SYHA hostels (managed by the Gatliff Hebridean Hostels Trust) are at Kershader and at **Gearranan** (10), the latter being one of the restored blackhouses.

PUBLIC TRANSPORT

There are frequent bus services on most of all the A and B roads, covering just about all possible destinations on the island. Most routes operate at least three times per day from Stornoway. The W10 route connects with Tarbert and South Harris.

Postbuses operate between Stornoway and Timsgarry and between Callanish and Bernera. Lewis people are strict observers of the Sabbath so nothing operates on a Sunday.

Stornoway has a few taxi services and vehicles may be hired (try Arnol Car Rentals, telephone 0800 328 5087). There are all sorts of tours on offer, from sightseeing coach tours to bird-watching, whale-watching and fishing trips.

ORDNANCE SURVEY LANDRANGER MAPS

Landranger sheets 8, 13, and 14 are required to cover all of Lewis. Sheet 8 is enough for Stornoway, North Lewis and most of the important archaeological sites.

MAIN PLACES OF INTEREST

Arnol Blackhouse (1) Traditional thatched blackhouse and museum at Arnol.

'Bridge to Nowhere' (2) Short Walk 26

Butt of Lewis (3) Walk 25

Butt of Lewis Lighthouse (4) Walk 25

Callanish Standing Stones and Circles (5) Short Walk 24

Clach an Truisel (6) At 5.7 m/$18^1/_2$ ft high, the largest single standing stone in Scotland, at Ballantrushal, GR 376537

Dun Carloway Broch (7) Best-preserved broch in Scotland (with the exception of Mousa Broch, Shetland). Walls stand up to 9 m/30 ft high – shows exceptional skills of Iron Age stone masons. Walk to a hilltop cairn at 84 m (GR 191414) to see Dun Carloway at its best

Dùn Othail (8) Short Walk 26

Garry Beach (9) Short Walk 26

Gerrannan Village (10) Short Walk 25

Glen Valtos (11) Walk 24; an oddity on Lewis, a lovely green steep-sided valley

Great Bernera (12) A 'bridge across the Atlantic' gives access to this scenic and fascinating island of Loch Ròg. There is a Norse mill, standing stones, an Iron Age village and a museum

Lews Castle (13) Short Walk 23

Loch Ròg (14) Walk 24

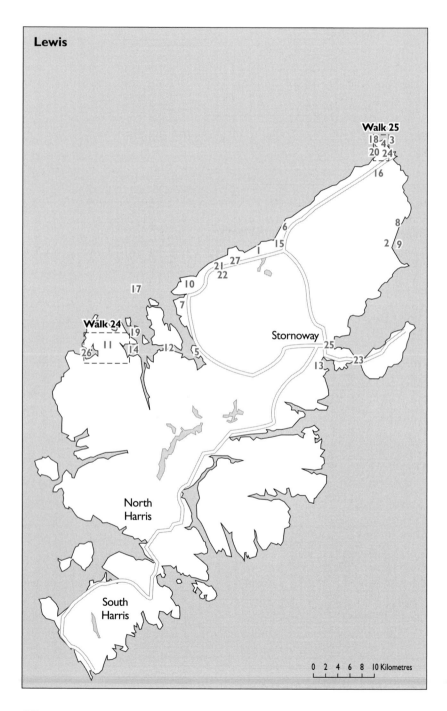

Lewis

Walk 25

18 3
4
20 24

16

6
15   8
1   2 9
21 27
22
10
17
7
Walk 24
19
26 11 14 12
5
Stornoway
25
13   23

North
Harris

South
Harris

0 2 4 6 8 10 Kilometres

Morven Gallery (15) Art and craft exhibitions and coffee shop at Barvas

Ness Museum (16) Habost

North Lochs (17) Scenic sea lochs frequented by whales

'Pygmy's Isle' (18) Walk 25

Reef Sands (**Tràigh na Beirigh**) (19) Superb beach, near Uig

Shanday Beach (20) Walk 25

Shawbost Crofting Museum (21) Shawbost (Siabost)

Shawbost Norse Mill and Kiln (22) Restored Norse mill and grain kiln

St Columba's Church (23) Ruins of early church and the ancient grave-yard of the MacLeods of Lewis, located at Aignish

St Moluag's Church (24) Walk 25

Stornoway (25) Largest town in the Hebrides with much of interest, including art gallery, museum castle, library, sports centre, fish market and a number of interesting churches. There are many shops and cafés. (see also Main Settlements and Short Walk 23)

Uig Sands (26) Walk 24

Whalebone Arch (27) Made from the huge jawbone of a blue whale, at Bragar

Farmhouse, Great Bernera, Lewis

Uig Sands and
Glen Valtos

Main interest and sights	Probably the most beautiful beach on Lewis and an impressive narrow canyon with SSSI status: Uig Sands (Tràigh Uuige) (26) Glen Valtos (Gleann Bhaltois) (11) Loch Ròg (14)
Route	Circular
Grade	Moderate
Map	OS Landranger sheet 13
Starting point	Car park behind the dunes at Uig Sands, GR 048328
Finishing point	As above
Distance	12.3 km/7$^1/_2$ mi (4$^3/_4$ hours)
Paths and terrain	Mostly good paths to Mavag (Miabhaig) but less so on south side of Glen Valtos. One short, steep descent and ascent. Some tarmac
Options	As an alternative to distant views there is a good case for walking all the way back through Glen Valtos on the road through the bottom of the cutting, to appreciate fully the confined, intimate drama of the place (easy/moderate, 4$^1/_4$ hours)
Nearby walks	None; nearest is Short Walk 26
Refreshments	Baile-na-cille Hotel at Timsgarry

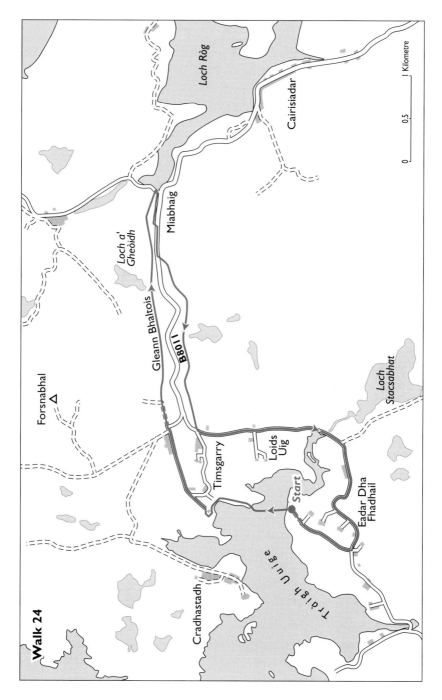

On a fine summer's evening, no sunset in the Hebrides can compare with the experience at Uig Bay (Camas Uig). Gaze westwards on a late summer evening from a perch on the dunes behind wide and spectacular tidal flats, and you will see the glancing sunlight cause banks of pale shell sand to glow acid orange. At such times, the place is a blaze of unreal fiery hues. Less poetically, but more famously, these sands were, for over 700 years, successful in hiding a unique collection of Norse relics. Different again, yet close by, is a fascinating 'glen in miniature' that cuts across the peninsula from west to east. This walk explores these many varied aspects of the Uig area, to my mind encompassing the most beautiful scenery to be found on Lewis.

The **Uig Sands** (26) are on the Atlantic fringe of the most mountainous part of Lewis, so, with the high grey, heather-covered mounds of Mealisval (Mealaisbhal), Tahaval (Tahabhal) and Suainaval (Suaineabhal), the beach enjoys a marvellous backdrop when seen from the north. Looking seaward, perhaps you will find a lover, for tales of marriage between island folk and mermaids or mermen are not uncommon in this part of Lewis.

Set off at low tide from the public conveniences behind the beach. It was in the dunes near here that in 1831 a crofter uncovered the 'Lewis Chessmen', the most famous of all Norse relics to have been discovered in the Hebrides. This twelfth-century collection of 78 walrus-ivory chess pieces (now divided between the British Museum in London and the Museum of Scotland in Edinburgh) is remarkable for the intricacy of their carvings, no two pieces being exactly alike. One can only guess as to the nature of the game of which the pieces were a part, whether it resembled at all what we today call chess. A local belief suggests that these carved images are in fact the gods of sailors rescued from a shipwreck.

Walk across the sands to the north then go over the footbridge and along as far as the picturesque burial ground below the hotel. Seafarers intending to continue west from here be warned: the Baile-na-Cille Hotel claims to have the 'last food and accommodation before Kennebunk, Maine, USA'.

Up along the road northeast of the hotel, walk past the school and on to the track that soon joins with the path above the north side of **Glen Valtos** (11). Follow that path eastwards to the far end of the glen. There are some fine cliff-top views along the way, looking down on the river and the strip of tarmac that both manage somehow to wriggle their way through this confined natural pass. Glen Valtos is a glacial meltwater channel that connects Camus Uig with **Loch Ròg** (14). The glen has been designated an SSSI, primarily because it is unique in the Western Isles in terms of size. The steep-sided drama of Glen Valtos is impressive yet small-scale.

From the corner of a line of rusty fencing above Loch Ròg, descend towards the wreck of a boat by its shore. Turn west and head back beside the Abhainn Ghlinne for 300 m, then cross the river to gain the road. From the B8011, vertiginous crags rise high on either side.

After a further 500 m/^{1}/$_3$ mi along the road, climb above the tarmac on a path heading towards the top corner of a tree plantation on the left. The situation is less claustrophobic again although for continuing drama keep as close to the edge as nerves allow. Walk behind the trees, heading west before finally coming down across unpathed moorland to meet the road. The walk along the top of the south side of the glen is rewarded by a panorama extending from the Uig hills, across sand and out to sea.

The final section is straightforward: south, then west, then north, along the coast road via the attractive township of Ardroil (Eadar Dha Fhadhail).

Butt of Lewis

Main interest and sights	An exposed and rugged headland where a sandy cove and a medieval church offer welcome protection: Butt of Lewis (3) Lighthouse (4) Pygmy's Isle (Luchruben) (18) Shanday Beach (Tràigh Shanndaigh) (20) St Moluag's Church (Teampall Mholuaidh) (24)
Route	Circular
Grade	Easy
Map	OS Landranger sheet 8
Starting point	Butt of Lewis lighthouse, GR 520664
Finishing point	As above
Distance	7.3 km/4^1/$_2$ mi (2^3/$_4$ hours)
Paths and terrain	Easy, level ground throughout and some tarmac. Care required at the cliff edges. Gentle gradients
Options	A succession of sandy coves for a further 4 km/2^1/$_2$ mi along the coast southeast of Shanday beach can be explored at will. Each bay has a track close by, connecting it to the A857
Nearby walks	None; nearest is Short Walk 26
Refreshments	None en route; shop at Coig Peighinnean, and the Inn at Cros.

The **Butt of Lewis** (3) is a wind-buffeted, wave-lashed jumble of fragmented precipices and detached rock – the untamed extremity of the archipelago, where the weather is rarely anything but energetic and where the sea never stops boiling. However, this northernmost square mile of the Long Isle is jam-packed with interest: history and legend, large marine mammals and seabird colonies, sand dunes and wild flowers, and a medieval

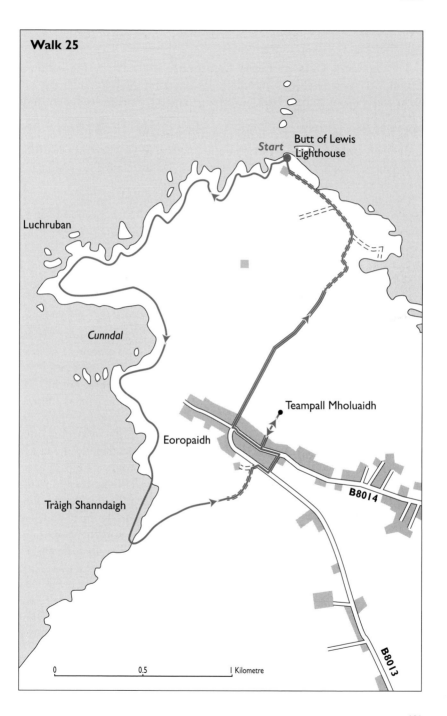

church and a lighthouse. All this in under three hours, on a headland dominated by a tempestuous sea.

The red-brick **Butt of Lewis Lighthouse** (4), built by the engineer David Stevenson, has been a distinctive landmark on the Butt for almost 140 years and remains an important beacon for shipping. Starting from here, simply follow the coast southwest, as close to the cliff edge as you can safely get. Wandering in and out over all the promontories and around the numerous little inlets is the best way to explore this coast, to experience the unceasing excitement happening below. Without pause waves crash into crumbling rock stacks, then surge through precipitous chasms.

On calmer days, in the spring and summertime, there is always good bird-watching on the Butt of Lewis. The cliffs then are the scene of a flurry of activity, with breeding colonies of cormorants, fulmars and kittiwakes. Gannets are also frequently seen, fishing farther out, hitting the water at great speed, wings swept back and beak pointing spear-like for the next fish. It is always possible to catch a sight of seals or dolphins or, if you are really lucky, a whale's back breaking the surface.

Before turning south to the Bay of Cunndal, notice the rock stack known as **Pygmy's Isle** (**Luchruban**) (18). Perhaps you can just make out the remains of a tiny kirk on top, said to have been the work of a pygmy race who once inhabited the little island. At low tide you can scramble up to it.

Approaching dune-backed **Shanday Beach** (**Tràigh Shanndaigh**) (20), there is more in the way of colour, a machair marked by the lines of cultivation ridges but also splashed with yellow trefoils, white clovers, sea pinks and purple orchids. Go over the stiles to reach the beach, normally a welcome sandy refuge away from the relentless wind. East of the dunes, behind the beach, there is a track across the grass to the settlement of Eoropie (Eoropaidh).

From the B8014, a path leads up through a yellow sea of buttercups to the twelfth-century **St Moluag's Church** (24). The present Episcopal chapel has undergone renovation and is still in use, with services on the first Sunday of every month. The door is usually left open, allowing visitors to enjoy its delightful interior. It was in the seventeenth century, however, that the church enjoyed its most popular era. The sick people of the island came here seeking divine intervention – to ensure the miraculous cure of any ailments, a visit, they believed, was enough. Teampall Ronaidh, dedicated to St Ronan who came to Lewis in early Christian days, once stood nearby on a mound to the east. It is said he grew desperate when he found an island of angry, argumentative people and had to summon a violent storm before they would be quiet.

From the crossroads at Eoropie, follow the road northwards, back to the lighthouse.

Short Walks

23 THE CASTLE GROUNDS, STORNOWAY (2 HOURS; OSLR MAP 8)

This walk is unique in the Western Isles because it explores a large tract of deciduous woodland. Lady Lever Park, **Stornoway** (25), constitutes the leafy environs of **Lews Castle** (13) and is wonderful in June when the rhododendrons are out. At any time it is ideal for spending a couple of hours, while waiting for the ferry perhaps. Besides the route suggested, there are a maze of other paths you could wander along. There are also Ranger-led walks every Saturday (telephone 01851 702002).

Lews Castle, an attractive building overlooking the harbour, was built by the Mathesons in the nineteenth century. The main building is now empty and rundown. Beginning from the castle, cross the Allt nam Brog and walk down to Shore Road. Follow the track along the shore as far as Greeta Island and then head upstream of the Greeta River as far as Memorial Fountain. From there, walk up to Gallows Hill, traditionally the site where criminals were executed, to admire the view.

24 CALLANISH (CALANAIS) STANDING STONES (1³/₄ HOURS; OSLR MAP 8 OR 13)

The 4,000-year-old stone circle of Callanish is probably the best-known visitor attraction in the Western Isles. Of all Britain's 900 or so ancient circles, it is second only to Stonehenge in importance. The astronomical alignment of the Wiltshire stones, however, relate to the sun whereas the **Callanish Standing Stones and Circles** (5) appear to relate to the cycles of the moon.

Fortunately, the enigma surrounding the Callanish site has not been compromised too much by a commercialism that attracts over 40,000 visitors a year, except that it is difficult to be alone there. Raised on a ridge overlooking Loch Ròg, the site consists of a series of stone rows radiating outward from the main circle of stones. Overall, the arrangement forms the shape of a cross, 123 m from north to south. But one of the most impressive aspects of the site is the special way in which the vertical stones of local gneiss (the tallest stands $4^1/_2$ m/$14^3/_4$ ft high) seem to shimmer and reflect the light, accentuating the atmosphere of mystery. As with other Neolithic circles, the site's exact purpose remains unknown so it is not surprising that many folk stories have grown up around the stones. In the seventeenth century, the people of Lewis called the stones Fir Bhreige ('False Men') as they were said to be the old giant inhabitants of Lewis turned to stone by St Kiaran because they refused to become Christian.

The walk begins at the Visitor Centre. Having visited the main circle of stones, continue to the crofting township of Callanish. From there follow the road east for 1 km/²/₃ mi, to the A858. A little farther on there are two smaller stone circles, Cnoc Cean a' Ghàrraidh and Cnoc Fhillibhir Bheag, on the right-hand side of the road. A path connects this pair. Go back along the road to return to the Callanish car park.

25 GEARRANNAN BLACKHOUSE VILLAGE AND TIUMPAN HEADLAND (1 ¹/₄ HOURS; OSLR MAP 8)

Half a dozen or so of the group of traditional thatched cottages at **Gearrannan Village** (**Na Gearrannan**) (10) have recently been restored, offering twenty-first-century visitors an insight into how nineteenth- and early twentieth-century crofters once lived. Apart from Arnol Blackhouse Museum, which still has a central peat fire in the kitchen and no chimney, the buildings at Gearrannan are the best examples of their kind on Lewis. One is now a visitor centre and shop, another a youth hostel whilst others are holiday homes.

From this 'restored' part of the settlement, located just above a stony beach, follow green and yellow marker posts northwards to Aird Mhòr. This is the summit perched above the headland at Tiumpan. Northeast and southwest, the coast is spectacular in both directions. Marker posts plot a route all the way to Dail Mòr if you wish to carry on farther eastwards. Otherwise, skirt around the east side of Aird Mhòr and from there return to the village. The marker posts are regained beyond a stile over some sheep fencing.

26 GARRY BEACH AND DÙN OTHAIL (2 ¹/₂ HOURS; OSLR MAP 8)

Garry Beach (**Tràigh Ghearadha**) (9) and neighbouring Big Beach (Tràigh Mhòr) vie with Uig Beach (Walk 24) as the most attractive stretch of sand on Lewis. Tràigh Ghearadha and Tràigh Mhòr lack the mountainous backdrop of Uig but in another way are more unusual because long sandy beaches are so rare on the east coast of Lewis. This walk traverses soft and peaty as well as firm and sandy terrain, and explores different types of coastal scenery and wildlife habitats.

Park at the car park at the north end of Big Beach (GR 534492) and walk northwards, behind the machair, to the road's terminus at the Garry River (Abhainn Ghearadha). You will pass above two prominent rock stacks on the way, both projecting from the sands. On one rest the remains of Mormaer's Castle (Caisteal a' Mhorair). The bridge spanning the Garry River, the

'**Bridge to Nowhere**' (2), was built at the start of a scheme to continue the coast road to Nis. Alas, this never actually materialised. The foundations were laid only as far as the Abhainn na Cloich, now a track that provides pleasant walking.

Continue north for about 1 km/²/₃ mi from this second river, following marker posts over spongy, wet moorland to shieling hut remains located close to a diminutive headland. Bear right towards the cliff edge to view **Dùn Othail** (8), impressive not for what still stands of the antiquity but for the heather-covered sea stack itself. This vertical column of rock is clinging on to the rest of Lewis just by a tether of gneiss at its base. On either side there are fine views along this sheltered coast as well as to the mainland on the eastern skyline. Peregrine falcons are known to breed on these cliffs.

Return as for the outward route, with the option of dropping down on to the sands of Garry Beach from the car park by the mouth of the river. Following the waymarked route over the dunes of Big Beach is a rewarding extension.

Black houses at Gearrannan

Other Islands to Visit

Five other islands of the northern Hebrides and beyond are, I feel, un doubtedly worthy of inclusion. Whether scenic or otherwise, their interest is more specific, and while they do not have the same potential for walking as those described in Chapter 7, they are nevertheless worth visiting.

MUCK

Muck is the smallest of the Small Isles, a gentle green low-lying island that frequently enjoys the sunniest weather of the four. Muck is a mantle of basalt with a fertile skin of shell sand overlain with green grass. There is no peat on the island, which means the 30 or so residents must import all their fuel.

Muck is a place without cars or, indeed, much else of the cares of civilisation. What it does have in abundance are wild flowers, such as marigold, cornflower and bluebell as well as alpine plants such as mountain cat's-paw and rose root sedum, which here grow 500 m/1,640 ft or more below their usual altitude.

There are attractive sandy beaches and seabirds, including puffins nesting on the cliffs close to the Spichean, a prominent rock pinnacle on the west side of Camas Mor. Muck is not for strenuous activities, more a place to completely unwind. There is a guesthouse at Port Mor and cottages for rent. Access is by Hebridean Cruises from Arisaig or the Cal Mac passenger ferry from Mallaig.

CANNA

Canna is distinctive because of its elevated plateau. With marvellous views to Rum and Skye the superb situation of the island is one of its main attractions. There are also pleasant pockets of deciduous woodland, especially above the harbour surrounding Canna House. Formerly the home of the renowned scholar Dr John Lorne Campbell, the house is interesting for its extensive library of Celtic literature and collection of Gaelic songs. This property and the rest of the island are owned by the NTS.

The charming little Protestant church above the harbour is, of the two churches, the one best looked after, surprising, perhaps, given the Catholic faith of the islanders. There are delightful coastal and cliff walks, and the ascent of its highest hills is easy. Compass Hill overlooks the east coast and the harbour, so named because of the compass-deflecting properties (iron) in the rock. Canna is made up of some extremely fertile soil on which some of the earliest crops in the West Highlands grow, giving it its other name, the 'Garden of the Hebrides'.

Canna Harbour is the best protected and most suitable in the Small Isles for ferry landings. The Cal Mac passenger ferry from Mallaig, the *Loch Nevis*, includes Canna in its itinerary. From Arisaig, access is by charter only. The NTS Resident Warden (telephone 01687 2477) may be able to arrange overnight accommodation; alternatively, bring your own tent.

BENBECULA

Benbecula and the Uists are in a sense one and the same place, a causeway from the north end of Benbecula joining it to North Uist and another causeway at its south end joining it to South Uist. Thus, the A865 links all three.

Benbecula has much of the wildlife and character of its neighbours without quite the same opportunity for walking. There is a mixed population of Catholics and Protestants, being as it is the transitional island between the two beliefs in the Western Isles.

The island is flat, low-lying and windswept, with numerous freshwater lochs. There is just one hill of any significance, Rueval 124 m/390 ft, the climb to its summit being the best walk on the island. There are two options: by the track going east from the A865 at Market Stance (Stansa na Fèille) or from Kyles of Flodda (Caola Fhlodaigh) to the north.

Historical sites include the ruins of fourteenth-century Nunton Chapel (OS Landranger sheet 8, GR 766537) and the remnant of Borne Castle (GR 773506), once a Clan Ranald stronghold.

HANDA

Handa is uninhabited, except by seabirds. Between May and August, razorbills, guillemots, kittiwakes, fulmars, puffins and other gulls and auks are present in their tens of thousands. It is for this reason alone that Handa receives the majority of its 5,000 a year visitors.

Handa lies far to the east of Lewis, just off mainland Sutherland and about 20 or so miles south of Cape Wrath. The remarkable monolithic mountains of Assynt are well seen from Handa with which it shares the same Torridonian sandstone geology. In early summer, birds' nests occupy every available ledge on cliffs rising to 120 m/394 ft above the sea. Guano covers much of the remaining exposed rock while a 3 sq km/1sq mi (309 ha/764 acre) turf of heather, moss and rough grass carpets the rest of the island. The peat bog in the vicinity of the ruined chapel was deep enough to have once been the burial ground of the dead from the mainland, to prevent their corpses being scavenged by wolves.

The most impressive feature of the island's cliffs is the Great Stack, a detached, flat-topped pinnacle of sandstone in the north. A sea-worn blowhole known as Poll Ghlup is close by. Handa is an excellent base for whale-watching as from here orca, minke and humpback whales may be seen. Dolphins and porpoises are also a common sight. There is a well-maintained, waymarked path for a 3–4 hour walk right around the island.

Befitting its status as a bird sanctuary and a Site of Special Scientific Interest, Handa was previously managed by the RSPB, but the owners, the Cadbury family (the chocolate people), felt that the Scottish Wildlife Trust offered a more enlightened attitude regarding the island's future. The SWT became the new managers in 1991.

Access is seasonal, by a small boat that plies the narrow Sound of Handa from Tarbet or on excursions from Scourie. Overnight stays are occasionally possible in the Assistant Warden's bothy.

ST KILDA

St Kilda is the farthest outlying group of islands in Scotland, some 70 km/44 mi out to sea due west of the Outer Hebrides. Their collective name is also given to Hirta, the largest island of the group, which boasts the highest sea cliffs (430 m/1,410 ft) in the British Isles. But St Kilda is special for many reasons.

Archaeological sites on Hirta, such as a Bronze Age ecclesiastical structure, a pre-Viking settlement and the more recently used cottages above Village Bay, are some of the stone-built legacies of its social history. Much has been written of St Kilda's community, of a people who had lived in virtual isolation for more than a 1,000 years. A 'parliament' of men would meet each day to decide on the day's work and the order of tasks, which invariably involved the gathering from the cliffs of seabirds for food. In carrying out this harvest, known as 'fowling', St Kildans developed highly skilled rock-climbing abilities.

In the nineteenth and early twentieth centuries the population of Hirta gradually declined, possibly in part because of the islanders' habit of rubbing guano into the navels of newborn children. The arrival of Victorian tourists introduced the trappings of civilisation, and they brought with them disease, aggravating the situation. The last 36 residents departed Hirta in 1930. With the exception of a missile-tracking radar station and NTS working parties, St Kilda has been left to the birds.

That gannets and puffins formed such an important part of the islanders' diet and that there was such a ready supply of fulmar oil for lighting is evidence of the abundance of seabirds on St Kilda. In both number and species terms, St Kilda has more seabirds than any other island group in northwest Europe. Stac Lee has possibly the largest gannetry in the world. Among resident creatures, both the St Kilda wren and the St Kilda fieldmouse are unique subspecies.

Owned by the NTS, the St Kilda archipelago boasts a list of impressive accolades: National Scenic Area, Ancient Monument and World Heritage Site, to name but three. However, seismic surveying of the seas surrounding St Kilda by major oil companies, greedy for the untapped reserves of black gold in what is known as the 'North Atlantic Frontier', continues unabated. Despite memories of recent environmental tragedies, the *Sea Empress*, the *Braer*, perhaps nothing has been learned?

There are cruises to St Kilda on boats that rarely land. The only way to enjoy an extended stay is to participate in a NTS summer working party for the repair and restoration of historic buildings on Hirta.

Black-backed gull

Glossary of Gaelic terms

aber mouth of loch, river
abhainn river
allt stream
aonach ridge
auch, ach field
bal, bail town, homestead
ban white, fair, pale
bealach hill pass
beg, beag small
ben, beinn hill
bhuidhe yellow
bidean pinnacle
blar plain
brae, braigh upper slope, steepening
breac speckled
cam cam
cairn pile of stones, often marking a
    summit
carn cairn, cairn-shaped hill
caol strait (kyle)
ceann, kin, ken head
ciche, cioch breast, breast-shaped hill
cil, kil church,cell
clach stone
cnoc hill, knoll
coillie, killie wood
corrie, coire, choire mountain, hollow
creag, craig cliff, crag
dal, dail field, flat
damh stag
dearg red
druim, drum long ridge
dubh, dhu black, dark
dun hill fort
eas waterfall
eilean island
eilidh hind
eun bird
fada long
fionn white
fraoch heather

gabhar, ghabhar, gobhar goat
garbh rough
geal white
gearr short
glen, gleann narrow valley
glias, glas grey
gorm blue, green
inch, inis island, meadow by river
inver, inbhir confluence
lag, laggan hollow
larach old site
lairig broad pass
leac slab
liath grey
loch lake (diminutive: lochan)
mam pass, rise
maol bare or bald (normally refers to
    mountain top without vegetation)
meall mound
monadh upland
mór(e) big
odhar, odhair dun-coloured
rhu, rubha point
riabhach brindled or striped
ruadh red, brown
sgor, sgurr pointed
sneachd snow
sron nose
stob pointed
strath valley (wider than glen)
tarmachan ptarmigan
tarsuinn transverse, across
tom hillock (rounded)
torr hillock (more rugged)
tulloch, tulach knoll
uaine green, pallid
uisge water, river

Useful Names, Addresses and Telephone Numbers

TOURIST BOARDS

Scottish Tourist Board
Central Information
23 Ravelston Terrace
Edinburgh EH4 3EU
Tel. (0131) 332 2433

Highlands of Scotland Tourist Board
Tourist Information Centre
Aviemore
Inverness-shire PH22 1PP
Tel. (0990) 143070

Western Isles Tourist Board
26 Cromwell Street
Stornoway
Isle of Lewis HS1 2DD
Tel. (01851) 703088

FERRY SERVICES AND EXCURSIONS

Caledonian MacBrayne Ltd
The Ferry Terminal
Gourock PA19 1QP
Tel. (01475) 650100
Reservations: Tel. (0990) 650000

Bella Jane Boat Trips (Elgol to
    Loch Coruisk, Skye)
Elgol, by Broadford
Isle of Skye IV49 9BJ
Tel. (01471) 866244

Eriksay Car Ferry
Tel. (01878) 720261

Hebridean Cruises (Small Isles)
Arisaig Harbour
Inverness-shire PH39 4NH
Tel. (01687) 450224

Glenelg to Kylerkea Ferry (Skye)
Tel. (01599) 511302

Sound of Barra Ferry
Tel. (01878) 720238/265

BUS SERVICES

Royal Mail (Postbuses)
7 Strothers Lane
Inverness IV1 1AA
Tel. (01463) 256200

National Express (Enquiry line)
Tel. (0990) 808080

Skyeways Travel
Tel. (01599) 534 328

Scottish Citylink Coaches
Buchanan Bus Station
Killermont Street
Glasgow G2 3NP
Tel. (0990) 505050

Macdonald coaches (Inverness to
    Ullapool)
Tel. (01851)706267

Hebridean Coaches
Tel. (01875) 235345/304

MAINLAND RAIL SERVICES (TO OBAN, MALLAIG AND KYLE)
Scotrail
Tel. (0345) 484950

INTER-ISLAND FLIGHTS (CONNECT WITH GLASGOW AND INVERNESS)
British Airways Express/Loganair
Tel. (0345) 222111

HOSTEL AND BUNKHOUSE ACCOMMODATION
Scottish Youth Hostels Association
  (SYHA)
7 Glebe Crescent
Stirling FK8 2JA
Tel. (01786) 451181

Independent Backpackers Hostels
  – Scotland (IBHS)
Pete Thomas
Croft Bunkhouse and Bothies
Portnalong
Isle of Skye IV47 8SL
Tel. (01478) 640254

The Gatliff Hebridean Hostels Trust
30 Francis Street
Stornoway
Isle of Lewis HS1 2ND

GAELIC STUDIES
Sabhal Mor Ostaig
Teangue, Sleat
Isle of Skye IV44 8RQ
Tel. (01471) 844 373

MISCELLANEOUS
Forestry Commission (FC)
231 Costorphine Road
Edinburgh EH12 7AT
Tel. (0131) 334 0303

Mountaineering Council of Scotland
4a St Catherine's Road
Perth PH1 5SE
Tel. (01738) 638227

National Trust for Scotland (NTS)
5 Charlotte Square
Edinburgh EH2 4DU
Tel. (0131) 226 5922

Royal Society for the Protection of
  Birds (RSPB)
Scottish Headquarters
17 Regent Street
Edinburgh EH7 5BN
Tel. (0131) 557 3136

Scottish Natural Heritage (SNH)
12 Hope Terrace
Edinburgh EH9 2AS
Tel. (0131) 447 4784

Scottish Wildlife Trust (SWT)
Cramond House
Cramond Glebe Road
Edinburgh EH4 6NS
Tel. (0131) 312 7765

Ramblers Assocation Scotland
Kingfisher House
Old Mart Business Centre
Milnathort
KY13 9DA
Tel. (01577) 861 222